Chocolate

LOVER'S

Cookies & Brownies

PUBLICATIONS INTERNATIONAL, LTD.

Copyright © 1990 Publications International, Ltd.
All rights reserved. This book may not be reproduced or quoted in whole or in part by mimeograph or any other printed or electronic means, or for presentation on radio, television, videotape, or film without written permission from:

Louis Weber, C.E.O.
Publications International, Ltd.
7373 North Cicero Avenue
Lincolnwood, Illinois 60646

Permission is never granted for commercial purposes.

Recipe Development: Beatrice Ojakangas
Photography and Food Styling: Burke/Triolo Studio
Pewter tray on page 60 courtesy of Princess Table, Los Angeles.

Printed in Yugoslavia by Zrinski

h g f e d c b a

ISBN 0-88176-872-3

Library of Congress Catalog Card Number 90-60062

Pictured on front and back covers:

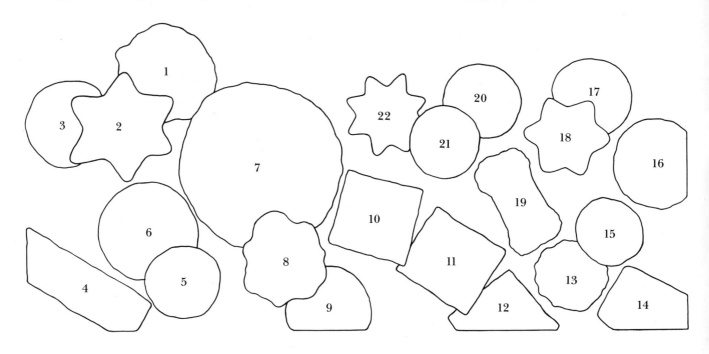

1 White Chocolate & Cocoa Chippers
  (*page 62*)
2 Cinnamon-Chocolate Cutouts (*page 79*)
3 Mrs. J's Chip Cookies (*page 63*)
4 Spumoni Bars (*page 80*)
5 Chocolate Tassies (*page 93*)
6 Chocolate Cookie Prints (*page 91*)
7 Peanut Butter Jumbos (*page 29*)
8 Aloha Chippers (*page 62*)

9 Double-Dipped Hazelnut Crisps
  (*page 83*)
10 White Chocolate & Almond Brownies
  (*page 38*)
11 Pecan Caramel Brownies (*page 35*)
12 Chocolate-Mint Brownies (*page 53*)
13 Whole Grain Chippers (*page 69*)
14 Orange & Chocolate Ribbon Cookies
  (*page 77*)

15 Chocolate-Mint Sandwiches (*page 78*)
16 Peanutty Double Chip Cookies (*page 63*)
17 Mocha Pecan Pinwheels (*page 72*)
18 Cinnamon-Chocolate Cutouts (*page 79*)
19 Chocolate Pistachio Fingers (*page 84*)
20 Mrs. J's Chip Cookies (*page 63*)
21 Chocolate Cherry Cookies (*page 73*)
22 Chocolate Spritz (*page 88*)

Chocolate LOVER'S
Cookies & Brownies

Chocolate Cookie Basics

One reason cookies and brownies have enjoyed such enduring popularity is that making them is as much fun as eating them. The following information on chocolate and on baking and storing cookies will enhance your chocolate-cookie-making fun.

TYPES OF CHOCOLATE

Unsweetened Chocolate: Also called bitter or baking chocolate, this is pure chocolate with no sugar or flavorings added. It is used only in baking and is commonly packaged in individually wrapped 1-ounce squares.

Bittersweet Chocolate: This is pure chocolate with some sugar added. Specialty food shops carry bittersweet chocolate in 1-ounce squares or in bars. If unavailable, substitute half unsweetened chocolate and half semisweet chocolate.

Semisweet Chocolate: Pure chocolate is combined with sugar and extra cocoa butter. It is sold in a variety of forms, including 1-ounce squares, bars, chips and chunks.

Milk Chocolate: This is pure chocolate with sugar, extra cocoa butter and milk solids added. It is available in various shapes—bars, chips, stars, etc.

White Chocolate: Also known as confectioners' or compound chocolate, this is not considered real chocolate since most or all of the cocoa butter has been removed and replaced by another vegetable fat. White chocolate is available in bars, blocks, disks, chips and chunks.

Unsweetened Cocoa: This is formed by extracting most of the cocoa butter from pure chocolate and grinding the remaining chocolate solids into a powder. It contains no additives.

MELTING CHOCOLATE

Make sure the utensils you use for melting are completely dry. Moisture makes the chocolate become stiff and grainy. If this happens, add ½ teaspoon shortening (not butter) for each ounce of chocolate and stir until smooth. Chocolate scorches easily, and once scorched it cannot be used. Follow one of these three methods for successful melting.

Double Boiler: This is the safest method because it prevents scorching. Simply place the chocolate in the top of a double boiler or in a bowl over hot, not boiling, water; stir until smooth.

Direct Heat: Place the chocolate in a heavy saucepan over very low heat. Stir constantly and remove from the heat as soon as it melts to prevent scorching.

Microwave Oven: Place an unwrapped 1-ounce chocolate square or 1 cup of chips in a small microwavable bowl. Microwave on High 1 to 1½ minutes, stirring after 1 minute. Be sure to stir microwaved chocolate since it holds its shape when melted. Times may differ with various oven wattages.

COOKIE-MAKING TIPS

• Read through the recipe and check the ingredients, pan sizes and any special requirements, such as chilling the dough. Be sure to measure all the ingredients accurately and always preheat the oven before baking.

• To easily shape drop cookies, use an ice cream scoop with a release bar. The bar usually has a number on it indicating the number of scoops that can be made from one quart of ice cream. The handiest size is a #80 to #90 scoop. This will yield about one rounded teaspoonful of dough for each cookie.

• When a recipe calls for greasing the cookie sheets, use shortening or a nonstick cooking spray for best results. Or, use parchment paper instead of greasing. It eliminates clean-up, bakes the cookies more evenly and allows them to cool right on the paper instead of on wire racks.

• For even baking and browning, bake cookies in the center of the oven. If heat distribution in your oven is uneven, turn the cookie sheet halfway through the baking time.

• Most cookies bake quickly and should be watched carefully to avoid overbaking. It is generally better to slightly underbake, rather than to overbake cookies.

STORING COOKIES

• Unbaked dough can be refrigerated for up to two weeks or frozen for up to six weeks. Rolls of dough should be sealed tightly in plastic wrap; other doughs should be stored in airtight containers. Label dough with baking information for convenience.

• Store soft and crisp cookies separately at room temperature. Use airtight containers for soft cookies and place an apple or bread slice in the container for a day if they begin to dry out. Store crisp cookies in containers with loose-fitting lids to prevent moisture buildup. If they become soggy, heat undecorated cookies in a 300°F oven for about 3 minutes to restore crispness.

• Store cookies with sticky glazes or fragile decorations in single layers. If dipped or edged with chocolate, they should be layered between sheets of waxed paper.

• Freeze baked cookies in airtight containers or freezer bags for up to 6 months. Unwrap cookies when thawing them. If soggy, crisp undecorated cookies in a 300°F oven for about 3 minutes. Meringue-based cookies do not freeze well and chocolate-dipped cookies will discolor if frozen.

Extra-Easy Cookies

Chocolate Sugar Drops (page 10), Chocolate-Coconut Cookies (page 10),
Chocolate & Peanut-Butter Tweed Cookies (page 11)

CHOCO-COCO PECAN CRISPS

½ cup butter or margarine, softened
1 cup packed light brown sugar
1 egg
1 teaspoon vanilla
1½ cups all-purpose flour
⅓ cup unsweetened cocoa
½ teaspoon baking soda
1 cup chopped pecans
1 cup flaked coconut

Cream butter and sugar in large bowl until blended. Beat in egg and vanilla. Combine flour, cocoa, baking soda and pecans in small bowl until well blended. Add to creamed mixture, blending until stiff dough is formed. Sprinkle coconut on work surface. Divide dough into 4 parts. Shape each part into a roll, about 1½ inches in diameter; roll in coconut until thickly coated. Wrap in plastic wrap; refrigerate until firm, at least 1 hour or up to 2 weeks. (For longer storage, freeze up to 6 weeks.) Preheat oven to 350°F. Line cookie sheets with parchment paper or leave ungreased. Cut rolls into ⅛-inch-thick slices; place 2 inches apart on ungreased cookie sheets. Bake 10 to 13 minutes or until firm, but not overly browned. Remove to wire racks to cool.

Makes about 6 dozen cookies

HOLIDAY FRUIT DROPS

½ cup butter, softened
¾ cup packed brown sugar
1 egg
1¼ cups all-purpose flour
1 teaspoon vanilla
½ teaspoon baking soda
½ teaspoon cinnamon
    Pinch salt
1 cup (8 ounces) diced candied pineapple
1 cup (8 ounces) red and green candied cherries
8 ounces chopped pitted dates
1 cup (6 ounces) semisweet chocolate chips
½ cup whole hazelnuts
½ cup pecan halves
½ cup coarsely chopped walnuts

Preheat oven to 325°F. Lightly grease cookie sheets or line with parchment paper. Cream butter and sugar in large bowl. Beat in egg until light. Mix in flour, vanilla, baking soda, cinnamon and salt. Stir in pineapple, cherries, dates, chocolate chips, hazelnuts, pecans and walnuts. Drop dough by rounded teaspoonfuls 2 inches apart onto prepared cookie sheets. Bake 15 to 20 minutes or until firm and lightly browned around edges. Remove to wire racks to cool.

Makes about 8 dozen cookies

Note: The hazelnuts, pecans and cherries are not chopped, but left whole.

Choco-Coco Pecan Crisps (left), Holiday Fruit Drops (right)

CHOCOLATE-COCONUT COOKIES

For a festive touch, top these easy-to-make cookies with red candied cherries and add them to your holiday cookie tray.

2 squares (1 ounce each) unsweetened chocolate
½ cup butter or margarine, softened
1 cup packed light brown sugar
1 egg
1¼ cups all-purpose flour
¼ teaspoon baking powder
⅛ teaspoon baking soda
  Dash salt
½ cup chopped walnuts or pecans
½ cup flaked coconut
  Pecan halves or halved red candied cherries

Preheat oven to 350°F. Lightly grease cookie sheets or line with parchment paper. Melt chocolate in top of double boiler over hot, not boiling, water. Remove from heat; cool. Cream butter and sugar in large bowl until blended. Add egg and melted chocolate; beat until light. Combine flour, baking powder, baking soda and salt in small bowl. Stir into creamed mixture until blended. Mix in nuts and coconut. Drop dough by teaspoonfuls 2 inches apart onto prepared cookie sheets. Press a pecan or cherry half into center of each cookie. Bake 10 to 12 minutes or until firm. Remove to wire racks to cool.

Makes 4 dozen cookies

CHOCOLATE SUGAR DROPS

Sugar cookies have never been easier! The dough is rolled into balls and flattened with the bottom of a glass dipped into sugar. Be sure to dip the glass into sugar before flattening each cookie.

½ cup butter or margarine, softened
½ cup vegetable oil
½ cup powdered sugar
½ cup granulated sugar
1 egg
2 cups all-purpose flour
¼ cup unsweetened cocoa
½ teaspoon baking soda
½ teaspoon cream of tartar
¼ teaspoon salt
1 teaspoon vanilla
  Granulated sugar

Cream butter, oil, powdered sugar, ½ cup granulated sugar and the egg in large bowl until light and fluffy. Combine the flour, cocoa, baking soda, cream of tartar and salt in small bowl. Add to creamed mixture with vanilla, stirring until dough is smooth. Cover; refrigerate 30 minutes or overnight, if desired.

Preheat oven to 350°F. Lightly grease cookie sheets or line with parchment paper. Shape dough into balls the size of marbles. Place 2 inches apart on prepared cookie sheets. Flatten each cookie to about ⅓-inch thickness with bottom of glass dipped into granulated sugar. Bake 10 minutes or until firm. Do not overbake. Remove to wire racks to cool.

Makes about 5 dozen cookies

CHOCOLATE & PEANUT-BUTTER TWEED COOKIES

The chopped chocolate and peanut butter chips in these cookies give them a tweedy texture and appearance.

1 cup butter or margarine, softened
½ cup packed light brown sugar
¼ cup granulated sugar
1 egg
¼ teaspoon baking soda
2½ cups all-purpose flour
½ cup *each* semisweet chocolate chips and peanut butter chips, chopped*

Cream butter and sugars in large bowl until smooth. Add egg and baking soda; beat until light. Stir in flour until dough is smooth. Blend in chopped chips. Divide dough into 4 parts. Shape each part into a roll, about 1½ inches in diameter. Wrap in plastic wrap; refrigerate until firm, at least 1 hour or up to 2 weeks. (For longer storage, freeze up to 6 weeks.)

Preheat oven to 375°F. Lightly grease cookie sheets or line with parchment paper. Cut rolls into ⅛-inch-thick slices; place 2 inches apart on prepared cookie sheets. Bake 10 to 12 minutes or until lightly browned. Remove to wire racks to cool.

Makes about 6 dozen cookies

*Chips can be chopped in a food processor.

HONEY-GINGER BOURBON BALLS

1 cup gingersnap cookie crumbs
1¼ cups powdered sugar, divided
1 cup finely chopped pecans or walnuts
1 square (1 ounce) unsweetened chocolate
1½ tablespoons honey
¼ cup bourbon

Combine crumbs, 1 cup of the sugar and the nuts in large bowl. Combine chocolate and honey in small bowl over hot water; stir until chocolate is melted. Blend in bourbon. Stir bourbon mixture into crumb mixture until well blended. Shape into 1-inch balls. Sprinkle remaining ¼ cup powdered sugar over balls. Refrigerate until firm.

Makes about 4 dozen balls

Note: These improve with aging. Store them in an airtight container in the refrigerator. They will keep several weeks, but are best after two to three days.

CHOCOLATE-FROSTED LEBKUCHEN

Lebkuchen are holiday favorites in Germany. The dough is traditionally baked on wafers called oblaten. You can find oblaten in some specialty food stores.

4 eggs
1 cup sugar
1½ cups all-purpose flour
1 cup (6 ounces) pulverized almonds*
⅓ cup candied lemon peel, finely chopped
⅓ cup candied orange peel, finely chopped
1½ teaspoons ground cinnamon
1 teaspoon grated lemon rind
½ teaspoon ground cardamom
½ teaspoon ground nutmeg
¼ teaspoon ground cloves
Bittersweet Glaze (recipe follows)

In large bowl of electric mixer, combine eggs and sugar. Beat at high speed for 10 minutes. Meanwhile, in separate bowl, combine flour, almonds, lemon and orange peels, cinnamon, lemon rind, cardamom, nutmeg and cloves. Blend in egg mixture, stirring until evenly mixed. Cover; refrigerate 12 hours or overnight.

Preheat oven to 350°F. Grease cookie sheets and dust with flour or line with parchment paper. Drop dough by rounded teaspoonfuls 2 inches apart onto prepared cookie sheets. Bake 8 to 10 minutes or until just barely browned. Do not overbake. Remove to wire racks. While cookies bake, prepare Bittersweet Glaze. Spread over tops of warm cookies using pastry brush. Cool until glaze is set. Store in airtight container.

Makes about 5 dozen cookies

*To pulverize almonds, place in food processor or blender. Process until thoroughly ground with a dry, not pasty, texture.

Melt chocolate and butter in small bowl over hot water. Stir until smooth.

BITTERSWEET GLAZE
3 squares (1 ounce each) bittersweet or semisweet chocolate, chopped
1 tablespoon butter or margarine

Chocolate-Frosted Lebkuchen, Honey-Ginger Bourbon Balls (page 11)

COCOA SNICKERDOODLES

Snickerdoodle is a nineteenth-century nonsense word for a quick-to-make confection. The dough is dropped into a mixture of cocoa, cinnamon and sugar, making the cookies crinkle when baked.

1 cup butter or margarine, softened
¾ cup packed brown sugar
¾ cup plus 2 tablespoons granulated sugar
2 eggs
2 cups uncooked rolled oats
1½ cups all-purpose flour
¼ cup plus 2 tablespoons unsweetened cocoa
1 teaspoon baking soda
2 tablespoons ground cinnamon

Preheat oven to 375°F. Lightly grease cookie sheets or line with parchment paper. Beat butter, brown sugar and the ¾ cup granulated sugar in large bowl until light and fluffy. Add eggs; mix well. Combine oats, flour, the ¼ cup cocoa and the baking soda in medium bowl. Stir into butter mixture until blended. Mix the 2 tablespoons granulated sugar, the cinnamon and the 2 tablespoons cocoa in small bowl. Drop dough by rounded teaspoonfuls into cinnamon mixture; toss to coat. Place 2 inches apart on prepared cookie sheets. Bake 8 to 10 minutes or until firm in center. Do not overbake. Remove to wire racks to cool.

Makes about 4½ dozen cookies

CHOCOLATE-PEANUT COOKIES

1 cup butter or margarine, softened
¾ cup granulated sugar
¾ cup packed light brown sugar
2 eggs
1 teaspoon vanilla
1 teaspoon baking soda
¼ teaspoon salt
2¼ cups all-purpose flour
2 cups chocolate-covered peanuts

Preheat oven to 375°F. Line cookie sheets with parchment paper or leave ungreased. Cream butter with sugars, eggs and vanilla in large bowl until light. Beat in baking soda and salt. Stir in flour to make stiff dough. Blend in chocolate-covered peanuts. Drop by rounded teaspoonfuls 2 inches apart onto cookie sheets. Bake 9 to 11 minutes or until just barely golden. Do not overbake. Remove to wire racks to cool.

Makes about 5 dozen cookies

Cocoa Snickerdoodles, Chocolate-Peanut Cookies

COWBOY COOKIES

Loaded with raisins, nuts and chocolate chips, these are a cookie-jar favorite that kids love!

½ cup butter or margarine,
  softened
½ cup packed light brown
  sugar
¼ cup granulated sugar
1 egg
1 teaspoon vanilla
1 cup all-purpose flour
2 tablespoons unsweetened
  cocoa
½ teaspoon baking powder
¼ teaspoon baking soda
1 cup uncooked rolled oats
1 cup (6 ounces) semisweet
  chocolate chips
½ cup raisins
½ cup chopped nuts

Preheat oven to 375°F. Lightly grease cookie sheets or line with parchment paper. Cream butter with sugars in large bowl until blended. Add egg and vanilla; beat until fluffy. Combine flour, cocoa, baking powder and baking soda in small bowl; stir into creamed mixture with oats, chocolate chips, raisins and nuts. Drop dough by teaspoonfuls 2 inches apart onto prepared cookie sheets. Bake 10 to 12 minutes or until lightly browned around edges. Remove to wire racks to cool.

Makes about 4 dozen cookies

BETH'S CHOCOLATE OATMEAL COOKIES

All butter or margarine may be used in place of the shortening in this recipe. The shortening, however, gives the cookies a more tender texture.

3 squares (1 ounce each)
  unsweetened chocolate
½ cup butter or margarine,
  softened
½ cup shortening
1½ cups sugar
2 eggs
2 teaspoons vanilla
1½ cups all-purpose flour
2 teaspoons baking powder
½ teaspoon salt
3 cups uncooked rolled oats
1 cup chopped walnuts

Preheat oven to 350°F. Lightly grease cookie sheets or line with parchment paper. Melt chocolate in top of double boiler over hot, not boiling, water. Remove from heat; cool. Cream butter, shortening and sugar in large bowl. Add eggs, beating well. Blend in melted chocolate and vanilla. Combine flour, baking powder and salt in small bowl. Add to creamed mixture; blend well. Mix in oats and nuts. Drop dough by rounded teaspoonfuls 2 inches apart onto prepared cookie sheets. Bake 10 to 12 minutes or until lightly browned. Remove to wire racks to cool.

Makes about 8 dozen cookies

Cowboy Cookies

ORIENTAL CHEWS

1 package (6 ounces) chow
  mein noodles
1 cup flaked coconut
1 cup (6 ounces) semisweet
  chocolate chips
1 cup (6 ounces)
  butterscotch-flavored
  chips
1 package (3 ounces)
  slivered almonds

Preheat oven to 350°F. Place noodles and coconut on cookie sheet in single layer. Bake 10 minutes or until crisp. Melt chocolate and butterscotch chips in top of double boiler over hot, not boiling, water. Remove from heat; stir in almonds, coconut and noodles. Drop mixture by teaspoonfuls onto waxed paper. Cool until set.

Makes about 5 dozen chews

MOCHA-WALNUT RUM BALLS

1 package (8½ ounces)
  chocolate cookie wafers
2 cups powdered sugar,
  divided
1¼ cups finely chopped
  toasted walnuts
2 tablespoons instant coffee
  granules
⅓ to ½ cup rum
2 tablespoons light corn
  syrup
½ teaspoon instant espresso
  coffee powder

Pulverize cookie wafers in food processor or blender to form powdery crumbs. Combine crumbs, 1½ cups of the sugar and the walnuts in large bowl. Dissolve coffee granules in ⅓ cup rum; stir in corn syrup. Blend into crumb mixture until crumbs are moistened enough to hold together. Add 2 to 3 tablespoons more rum, if necessary. Shape into 1-inch balls. Mix the remaining ½ cup sugar with the espresso coffee powder. Roll balls in sugar mixture to coat. Store loosely packed between sheets of waxed paper or foil in airtight container up to 2 weeks.

Makes about 100 balls

PEOPLE CHOW

Serve a generous bowlful of this chow to the nibblers in your crowd!

1 cup butter or margarine
1 package (12 ounces)
  semisweet chocolate
  chips
18 cups dry cereal (mixture of
  bite-sized wheat, corn
  and rice cereal squares
  or toasted oat cereal)
2 cups nuts (cashews,
  peanuts, mixed nuts,
  pecans or walnuts)
6 cups powdered sugar

Melt butter and chocolate chips in medium-sized heavy saucepan over low heat; stir to blend. Place cereal and nuts in large bowl. Pour chocolate mixture over; mix until cereal and nuts are thoroughly coated. Turn chocolate mixture into very large bowl or dishpan. Sprinkle sugar over, 2 cups at a time, carefully folding and mixing until thoroughly coated.

Makes about 24 cups

DATE FUDGE COOKIES

The dates in these cookies keep them fresh and moist for a long time.

1 cup (6 ounces) semisweet
　　chocolate chips
½ cup butter or margarine,
　　softened
1 cup granulated sugar
2 eggs
1½ cups all-purpose flour
　　Dash salt
1 package (8 ounces)
　　chopped pitted dates
½ cup coarsely chopped
　　pecans or walnuts
　　Brown-Sugar Icing (recipe
　　follows)

Preheat oven to 375°F. Lightly grease cookie sheets or line with parchment paper. Melt chocolate chips in top of double boiler over hot, not boiling, water. Remove from heat; cool. Cream butter, granulated sugar and eggs in large bowl until smooth. Beat in melted chocolate. Gradually add flour and salt, mixing until smooth. Stir in dates and nuts. Drop dough by rounded teaspoonfuls 2 inches apart onto prepared cookie sheets. Bake 10 to 12 minutes or until slightly firm. Cool 5 minutes on cookie sheets, then remove to wire racks. While cookies bake, prepare Brown-Sugar Icing. Spread over cookies while still warm. Cool until icing is set.

Makes about 5 dozen cookies

BROWN-SUGAR ICING
½ cup packed dark brown
　　sugar
¼ cup water
2 squares (1 ounce each)
　　unsweetened chocolate
2 cups powdered sugar
¼ cup butter or margarine
1 teaspoon vanilla

Combine brown sugar, water and chocolate in small heavy saucepan. Stir over medium heat until chocolate is melted and mixture boils. Boil 1 minute. Remove from heat, beat in powdered sugar, butter and vanilla. Continue beating until mixture has cooled slightly and thickened. Spread over cookies while icing is still warm.

CRISPY CHOCOLATE LOGS

1 cup (6 ounces) semisweet
　　chocolate chips
½ cup butter or margarine
1 package (10 ounces)
　　marshmallows
6 cups crispy rice cereal

Lightly oil a 13×9-inch baking pan. Melt chocolate chips and butter in large bowl over hot water, stirring constantly. Add marshmallows; stir until melted. Add cereal; stir until evenly coated with chocolate mixture. Press into prepared pan; cool until mixture is firm. Cut into 2×1½-inch logs using a sharp, thin knife.

Makes 36 logs

NUTTY CLUSTERS

2 squares (1 ounce each)
    unsweetened chocolate
½ cup butter or margarine,
    softened
1 cup granulated sugar
1 egg
⅓ cup buttermilk
1 teaspoon vanilla
1¾ cups all-purpose flour
½ teaspoon baking soda
1 cup mixed salted nuts,
    coarsely chopped
    Chocolate Icing (recipe
    follows)

Preheat oven to 400°F. Line cookie sheets with parchment paper or leave ungreased. Melt chocolate in top of double boiler over hot, not boiling, water. Remove from heat; cool. Cream butter and granulated sugar in large bowl until smooth. Beat in egg, melted chocolate, buttermilk and vanilla until light. Stir in flour, baking soda and nuts. Drop dough by teaspoonfuls 2 inches apart onto cookie sheets. Bake 8 to 10 minutes or until almost no imprint remains when touched. Immediately remove cookies from cookie sheet to wire rack. While cookies bake, prepare Chocolate Icing. Frost cookies while still warm.

Makes about 4 dozen cookies

CHOCOLATE ICING
2 squares (1 ounce each)
    unsweetened chocolate
2 tablespoons butter or
    margarine
2 cups powdered sugar
2 to 3 tablespoons water

Melt chocolate and butter in small heavy saucepan over low heat, stirring until completely melted. Add powdered sugar and water, mixing until smooth.

OAT & DRIED-FRUIT BALLS

3 cups uncooked rolled oats
1 cup flaked coconut
1 cup chopped dried mixed
    fruit
¼ cup sunflower seeds or
    chopped walnuts
1 cup sugar
½ cup milk
½ cup butter or margarine
6 tablespoons unsweetened
    cocoa
¼ teaspoon salt
1 teaspoon vanilla

Combine oats, coconut, fruit and sunflower seeds in large bowl; set aside. Combine sugar, milk, butter, cocoa and salt in 2-quart saucepan until blended. Heat to boiling. Boil 3 minutes, stirring constantly; remove from heat. Stir in vanilla. Pour hot sugar syrup into oat mixture; stir until well blended. When cool enough to handle, shape rounded tablespoonfuls into balls; place on waxed paper until completely cooled and firm.

Makes about 5 dozen balls

PEANUT-BUTTER CHOCOLATE STARS

1 cup peanut butter
1 cup packed light brown
    sugar
1 egg
48 milk chocolate candy stars
    or other solid milk
    chocolate candy

Preheat oven to 350°F. Line cookie sheets with parchment paper or leave ungreased. Combine peanut butter, sugar and egg in medium bowl until blended and smooth. Shape into 48 balls about 1½ inches in diameter. Place 2 inches apart on cookie sheets. Press a chocolate star onto the top of each cookie. Bake 10 to 12 minutes or until set. Remove to wire racks to cool.

Makes 4 dozen cookies

FUDGE COOKIES

Satisfying and rich with chocolate, these fudgy cookies are gilded with a good fudge frosting, too.

1 cup (6 ounces) semisweet
    chocolate chips
½ cup butter or margarine,
    softened
1 cup granulated sugar
2 eggs
1½ cups all-purpose flour
    Dash salt
1½ cups coarsely chopped
    pecans or walnuts
    Fudge Frosting (recipe
    follows)

Preheat oven to 375°F. Lightly grease cookie sheets or line with parchment paper. Melt chocolate chips in top of double boiler over hot, not boiling, water. Remove from heat; cool. Cream butter, granulated sugar and eggs in large bowl until smooth. Beat in melted chocolate. Gradually add flour and salt, mixing until smooth. Stir in nuts. Drop dough by rounded teaspoonfuls 2 inches apart onto prepared cookie sheets. Bake 10 to 12 minutes or until slightly firm. Cool 5 minutes on cookie sheet, then remove to wire racks. While cookies bake, prepare Fudge Frosting. Frost cookies while still warm. Cool until frosting is set.

Makes about 5 dozen cookies

FUDGE FROSTING
1 square (1 ounce)
    semisweet chocolate
3 tablespoons heavy cream
1 cup powdered sugar
1 teaspoon vanilla

Melt chocolate with cream in small heavy saucepan over medium heat, stirring until chocolate melts completely. Remove from heat; beat in powdered sugar and vanilla. Spread over cookies while frosting is still warm.

Fudge Cookies, Oat & Dried-Fruit Balls (page 20), Peanut-Butter Chocolate Stars

ICE CREAM COOKIES

These cookies are simple, buttery and chocolatey—perfect to serve alongside ice cream or to make into ice cream sandwiches.

2 squares (1 ounce each)
    unsweetened chocolate
1 cup butter, softened
1 cup powdered sugar
4 egg yolks
1 teaspoon vanilla
3 cups all-purpose flour
    Powdered sugar

Melt chocolate in top of double boiler over hot, not boiling, water. Remove from heat; cool. Cream butter and 1 cup sugar in large bowl until blended. Add egg yolks, vanilla and melted chocolate; beat until light. Blend in flour to make stiff dough. Divide dough into 4 parts. Shape each part into a roll, about 1½ inches in diameter. Wrap in plastic wrap; refrigerate until firm, at least 30 minutes or up to 2 weeks. (For longer storage, freeze up to 6 weeks.)

Preheat oven to 350°F. Line cookie sheets with parchment paper or leave ungreased. Cut rolls into ⅛-inch-thick slices; place 2 inches apart on ungreased cookie sheets. Bake 8 to 10 minutes or just until set, but not browned. Remove to wire racks to cool. Dust with powdered sugar.

Makes about 8 dozen cookies

Ice Cream Cookie Sandwiches: Prepare and bake cookies as directed; cool completely. Spread desired amount of softened ice cream on bottoms of half the cookies. Top with remaining cookies, bottom sides down, forming sandwiches. Dust tops with powdered sugar; serve immediately. Makes about 4 dozen sandwich cookies.

Ice Cream Cookie Sandwiches

Monster Cookies

Top left: White Chocolate Biggies (page 28), bottom left: Peanut Butter Jumbos (page 29)

WHITE CHOCOLATE BIGGIES

These huge chocolate cookies are studded with white chocolate chips, pecans and raisins. They bake to about four inches in diameter.

1½ cups butter or margarine, softened
1 cup granulated sugar
¾ cup packed light brown sugar
2 teaspoons vanilla
2 eggs
2½ cups all-purpose flour
⅔ cup unsweetened cocoa
1 teaspoon baking soda
½ teaspoon salt
1 package (10 ounces) large white chocolate chips
¾ cup pecan halves, coarsely chopped
½ cup golden raisins

Preheat oven to 350°F. Lightly grease cookie sheets or line with parchment paper. Cream butter, sugars, vanilla and eggs in large bowl until light. Combine flour, cocoa, baking soda and salt in medium bowl; blend into creamed mixture until smooth. Stir in white chocolate chips, pecans and raisins. Scoop out about ⅓ cupful of dough for each cookie. Place on prepared cookie sheets, spacing about 4 inches apart. Press each cookie to flatten slightly. Bake 12 to 14 minutes or until firm in center. Cool 5 minutes on cookie sheet, then remove to wire racks to cool completely.

Makes about 2 dozen cookies

CHOCOLATE PLATTER COOKIES

1 cup unsalted butter, softened
1 cup packed light brown sugar
½ cup granulated sugar
2 eggs
2⅓ cups all-purpose flour
1 teaspoon baking soda
½ teaspoon salt
1 package (12 ounces) semisweet chocolate chunks
2 cups chopped pecans

Preheat oven to 375°F. Lightly grease cookie sheets or line with parchment paper. Cream butter with sugars until smooth. Add eggs; beat until fluffy. Combine flour, baking soda and salt in small bowl. Add to creamed mixture, mixing until dough is stiff. Stir in chocolate chunks and pecans. Scoop out about ⅓ cupful of dough for each cookie. Place on prepared cookie sheets, spacing 4 inches apart. Using back of fork, flatten each cookie to about ½ inch thick. Bake 15 minutes or until light golden. Remove to wire racks to cool.

Makes about 16 cookies

PEANUT BUTTER JUMBOS

½ cup butter or margarine, softened
1 cup packed brown sugar
1 cup granulated sugar
1½ cups peanut butter
3 eggs
2 teaspoons baking soda
1 teaspoon vanilla
4½ cups uncooked rolled oats
1 cup (6 ounces) semisweet chocolate chips
1 cup candy-coated chocolate pieces

Preheat oven to 350°F. Lightly grease cookie sheets or line with parchment paper. Cream butter, sugars, peanut butter and eggs in large bowl until light. Blend in baking soda, vanilla and oats until well mixed. Stir in chocolate chips and candy pieces. Scoop out about ⅓ cupful of dough for each cookie. Place on prepared cookie sheets, spacing about 4 inches apart. Press each cookie to flatten slightly. Bake 15 to 20 minutes or until firm in center. Remove to wire racks to cool.

Makes about 1½ dozen cookies

GIANT RAISIN-CHIP FRISBEES

Decorate frisbees with candles for a birthday party—kids love them!

1 cup butter or margarine, softened
1 cup packed brown sugar
½ cup granulated sugar
2 eggs
1 teaspoon vanilla
1½ cups all-purpose flour
¼ cup unsweetened cocoa
1 teaspoon baking soda
1 cup (6 ounces) semisweet chocolate chips
¾ cup raisins
¾ cup chopped walnuts

Preheat oven to 350°F. Line cookie sheets with parchment paper or lightly grease and dust with flour. Cream butter with sugars in large bowl. Add eggs and vanilla; beat until light. Combine flour, cocoa and baking soda in small bowl. Add to creamed mixture with chocolate chips, raisins and walnuts; stir until well blended. Scoop out about ½ cupful of dough for each cookie. Place on prepared cookie sheets, spacing about 5 inches apart. Using knife dipped in water, smooth balls of dough out to 3½ inches in diameter. Bake 10 to 12 minutes or until golden. Remove to wire racks to cool.

Makes about 16 cookies

TRACY'S PIZZA-PAN COOKIES

Cream cheese adds flavor and a chewy texture to these pizza-sized cookies.

1 cup butter or margarine, softened
¾ cup granulated sugar
¾ cup packed brown sugar
1 package (8 ounces) cream cheese, softened
1 teaspoon vanilla
2 eggs
2¼ cups all-purpose flour
1 teaspoon baking soda
¼ teaspoon salt
1 package (12 ounces) semisweet chocolate chips
1 cup chopped walnuts or pecans

Preheat oven to 375°F. Lightly grease two 12-inch pizza pans. Cream butter, sugars, cream cheese and vanilla in large bowl. Add eggs; beat until light. Combine flour, baking soda and salt in small bowl. Add to creamed mixture; blend well. Stir in chocolate chips and nuts. Divide dough in half; press each half evenly into a prepared pan. Bake 20 to 25 minutes or until lightly browned around edges. Cool completely in pans on wire racks. To serve, cut into slim wedges or break into pieces.

Makes two 12-inch cookies

SUPER-DUPER CHOCOLATE PECAN COOKIES

½ cup butter or margarine, softened
⅓ cup peanut butter
⅓ cup granulated sugar
⅓ cup packed light brown sugar
1 egg
1 teaspoon vanilla
1¼ cups all-purpose flour
½ teaspoon baking soda
1 package (12 ounces) semisweet chocolate chunks *or* 4 semisweet chocolate bars (3 ounces each), cut into squares
1 cup pecan halves, cut into pieces

Preheat oven to 350°F. Lightly grease two cookie sheets or line with parchment paper. Cream butter, peanut butter, sugars, egg and vanilla in large bowl until light. Blend in flour and baking soda. Scoop out about ⅓ cupfuls of dough to form 12 balls. Place on prepared cookie sheets, spacing about 4 inches apart. Press each cookie to flatten slightly. Press chocolate chunks and pecan pieces into cookies, dividing them equally. Bake 15 to 17 minutes or until firm in center. Remove to wire racks to cool.

Makes 1 dozen cookies

Brownies & Bars

Left: Pecan Caramel Brownies (page 35), right: Chocolate Peanut Bars (page 34)

CHOCOLATE PEANUT BARS

½ cup butter or margarine,
  softened
¼ cup granulated sugar
1 cup packed brown sugar,
  divided
2 eggs, separated
1 teaspoon vanilla
2 cups all-purpose flour
2 teaspoons baking powder
½ teaspoon baking soda
¼ teaspoon salt
2 to 4 tablespoons milk
1 cup (6 ounces) semisweet
  chocolate chips
¾ cup salted peanuts,
  coarsely chopped

Preheat oven to 350°F. Lightly grease a 13×9-inch pan. Cream butter, granulated sugar and ¼ cup of the brown sugar in large bowl. Beat in egg yolks and vanilla. Combine flour, baking powder, baking soda and salt in small bowl. Blend into creamed mixture. Stir in enough milk to make a smooth, light dough. Press on bottom of prepared pan. Sprinkle chocolate chips over the top; press them down lightly into dough. In clean, dry bowl, beat egg whites until stiff, but not dry. Gradually beat in remaining ¾ cup brown sugar. Spread mixture evenly over dough in pan; top with peanuts. Bake 25 to 30 minutes or until top is puffed, lightly browned and feels dry. Cut into 2×1-inch bars while still warm.

Makes about 5 dozen bars

PEANUT-BUTTER-CHIP BROWNIES

½ cup butter or margarine
4 squares (1 ounce each)
  semisweet chocolate
½ cup sugar
2 eggs
1 teaspoon vanilla
½ cup all-purpose flour
1 package (12 ounces)
  peanut butter chips
1 cup (6 ounces) milk
  chocolate chips

Preheat oven to 350°F. Butter an 8-inch square pan. Melt butter and semisweet chocolate in small heavy saucepan over low heat, stirring just until chocolate melts completely. Remove from heat; cool. Beat sugar and eggs in large bowl until light. Blend in vanilla and chocolate mixture. Stir in flour until blended; fold in peanut butter chips. Spread batter evenly in prepared pan. Bake 25 to 30 minutes or just until firm and dry in center. Remove from oven; sprinkle milk chocolate chips over the top. Place pan on wire rack. When chocolate chips have melted, spread them over brownies. Refrigerate until chocolate topping is set. Cut into 2-inch squares.

Makes 16 brownies

PECAN CARAMEL BROWNIES

Pecans, caramel and chocolate make an irresistible combination.

50 caramel candy cubes
2 tablespoons milk
1½ cups granulated sugar
1 cup butter or margarine,
  melted
4 eggs
2 teaspoons vanilla
1 cup all-purpose flour
⅔ cup unsweetened cocoa
½ teaspoon baking powder
¼ teaspoon salt
1 cup (6 ounces) semisweet
  chocolate chips
⅓ cup pecan halves
  Cocoa Glaze (recipe
  follows)

COCOA GLAZE
2 tablespoons butter or
  margarine
2 tablespoons unsweetened
  cocoa
2 tablespoons milk
  Dash salt
1 cup powdered sugar
1 teaspoon vanilla

Preheat oven to 350°F. Butter a 13×9-inch pan. Unwrap caramels; melt with milk in small heavy saucepan over medium to low heat, stirring until caramels melt completely. Keep warm. Combine granulated sugar, butter, eggs, vanilla, flour, cocoa, baking powder and salt in large bowl. Beat with mixer at medium speed until smooth. Spread half of the batter in prepared pan. Bake 15 minutes. Carefully remove from oven; sprinkle with chocolate chips. Drizzle melted caramel mixture over the top, covering evenly. Spoon remaining batter over all. Return to oven; bake 20 minutes longer. Do not overbake. Meanwhile, toast pecan halves in another pan in same oven 3 to 5 minutes. Prepare Cocoa Glaze. Pour over warm brownies; arrange toasted pecans on top. Cool completely in pan on wire rack. Cut into 2-inch squares.

Makes about 2 dozen brownies

Combine butter, cocoa, milk and salt in small heavy saucepan. Bring to a boil over medium heat, stirring constantly. Remove from heat; add powdered sugar and beat until smooth. Stir in vanilla.

BROWNIE FUDGE

This recipe makes a huge batch of fudge-topped brownies—ideal to serve a crowd.

4 squares (1 ounce each)
    unsweetened chocolate
1 cup butter or margarine
2 cups sugar
4 eggs
1 cup all-purpose flour
1 cup chopped walnuts
2 teaspoons vanilla
    Fudge Topping (recipe
    follows)

Preheat oven to 350°F. Butter a 13×9-inch pan. Melt chocolate and butter in small heavy saucepan over low heat, stirring until completely melted; cool. Beat sugar and eggs in large bowl until light and fluffy. Gradually whisk chocolate mixture into egg mixture. Stir in flour, walnuts and vanilla. Spread batter evenly in prepared pan. Bake 25 to 35 minutes or just until set. Do not overbake. Meanwhile, prepare Fudge Topping. Remove brownies from oven. Immediately pour topping evenly over hot brownies. Cool in pan on wire rack. Place in freezer until firm. Cut into 1-inch squares.

Makes about 9 dozen brownies

FUDGE TOPPING

4½ cups sugar
⅓ cup butter or margarine
1 can (12 ounces) evaporated
    milk
1 jar (7 ounces) marshmallow
    creme
1 package (12 ounces)
    semisweet chocolate
    chips
1 package (12 ounces) milk
    chocolate chips
2 teaspoons vanilla
2 cups walnuts, coarsely
    chopped

Combine sugar, butter and milk in large saucepan. Bring to a boil over medium heat; boil 5 minutes, stirring constantly. Remove from heat; add remaining ingredients *except* walnuts. Beat until smooth. Stir in walnuts.

Left: White Chocolate & Almond Brownies (page 38), right: Brownie Fudge

WHITE CHOCOLATE & ALMOND BROWNIES

Use a high-quality white chocolate when you make these brownies. The white chocolate sweetens them so sugar is not needed in the recipe.

12 ounces white chocolate, broken into pieces
1 cup unsalted butter
3 eggs
¾ cup all-purpose flour
1 teaspoon vanilla
½ cup slivered almonds

Preheat oven to 325°F. Grease and flour 9-inch square pan. Melt chocolate and butter in large saucepan over low heat, stirring constantly. (Do not be concerned if the white chocolate separates.) Remove from heat when chocolate is just melted. With electric mixer, beat in eggs until mixture is smooth. Beat in flour and vanilla. Spread batter evenly in prepared pan. Sprinkle almonds evenly over the top. Bake 30 to 35 minutes or just until set in center. Cool completely in pan on wire rack. Cut into 2-inch squares.

Makes about 16 brownies

FUDGY FUDGE BROWNIES

Rich, moist and chewy, these brownies are for real chocolate lovers!

½ cup butter or margarine
2 squares (1 ounce each) unsweetened chocolate
2 eggs
1 cup granulated sugar
½ cup all-purpose flour
1 teaspoon vanilla
  Fudgy Frosting, optional (recipe follows)

Preheat oven to 325°F. Grease and flour an 8-inch square pan. Melt butter and chocolate in small heavy saucepan over low heat. Remove from heat; cool. Beat eggs in medium bowl until light and fluffy. Add granulated sugar, beating well. Blend in chocolate mixture. Stir in flour and vanilla. Spread batter evenly in prepared pan. Bake 30 minutes or until firm in center. Cool in pan on wire rack. Frost with Fudgy Frosting, if desired. Cut into 2-inch squares.

Makes 16 brownies

FUDGY FROSTING
2 squares (1 ounce each) unsweetened chocolate
½ cup heavy cream
1 cup granulated sugar
  Dash salt
1 teaspoon vanilla
½ to ¾ cup powdered sugar

Melt chocolate with cream in small heavy saucepan over low heat, stirring until chocolate melts completely. Stir in granulated sugar and salt. Bring to a boil. Boil 1 minute. Remove from heat; stir in vanilla. Beat until smooth. Add enough powdered sugar to make frosting a soft spreading consistency. Beat until slightly cooled; spread over brownies.

HEAVENLY HASH BROWNIES

This version of heavenly hash uses a combination of chocolate, nuts and marshmallows. For best results, be sure to use fresh marshmallows.

1 cup butter or margarine
¼ cup unsweetened cocoa
4 eggs
1¼ cups granulated sugar
1½ cups all-purpose flour
2 cups chopped walnuts or pecans
2 teaspoons vanilla
  Creamy Cocoa Icing (recipe follows)
1 package (10 ounces) miniature marshmallows

Preheat oven to 350°F. Grease a 13×9-inch pan. Melt butter in 2-quart saucepan; stir in cocoa. Remove from heat; beat in eggs and granulated sugar. Blend in flour, nuts and vanilla. Spread batter evenly in prepared pan. Bake 20 to 25 minutes or until center feels dry. Do not overbake. Meanwhile, prepare Creamy Cocoa Icing. Remove brownies from oven. Immediately sprinkle marshmallows over hot brownies. Pour hot icing evenly over marshmallows. Cool in pan on wire rack. Cut into 2-inch squares.

Makes about 2 dozen brownies

CREAMY COCOA ICING

6 tablespoons butter or margarine
¾ cup undiluted evaporated milk
6 cups powdered sugar
¾ cup unsweetened cocoa

Combine butter, milk, powdered sugar and cocoa in 2-quart saucepan. Stir over low heat until smooth and creamy.

COCONUT-ALMOND MOUND BARS

2 cups graham cracker crumbs
½ cup butter or margarine, softened
¼ cup powdered sugar
2 cups flaked coconut
1 can (14 ounces) sweetened condensed milk
½ cup whole blanched almonds
1 cup (6 ounces) milk chocolate chips

Preheat oven to 350°F. Lightly grease a 13×9-inch pan. Combine crumbs, butter and powdered sugar in large bowl until blended and smooth. Press on bottom of prepared pan. Bake 10 to 12 minutes or just until golden. Combine coconut and milk in small bowl; spread evenly over baked crust. Arrange almonds evenly over coconut mixture. Bake 15 to 18 minutes or until almonds are toasted. Remove from oven; sprinkle chocolate chips over the top. Let stand a few minutes until chips melt, then spread evenly over bars. Cool completely in pan on wire rack. Cut into 2×1½-inch bars.

Makes about 3 dozen bars

RASPBERRY FUDGE BROWNIES

½ cup butter or margarine
3 squares (1 ounce each) bittersweet chocolate*
2 eggs
1 cup sugar
1 teaspoon vanilla
¾ cup all-purpose flour
¼ teaspoon baking powder
Dash salt
½ cup sliced or slivered almonds
½ cup raspberry preserves
1 cup (6 ounces) milk chocolate chips

Preheat oven to 350°F. Butter and flour an 8-inch square pan. Melt butter and bittersweet chocolate in small heavy saucepan over low heat. Remove from heat; cool. Beat the eggs, sugar and vanilla in large bowl until light. Beat in chocolate mixture. Stir in flour, baking powder and salt until just blended. Spread ¾ of the batter in prepared pan; sprinkle almonds over the top. Bake 10 minutes. Remove from oven; spread preserves over almonds. Carefully spoon remaining batter over preserves, smoothing top. Bake 25 to 30 minutes or just until top feels firm. Remove from oven; sprinkle chocolate chips over the top. Let stand a few minutes until chips melt, then spread evenly over brownies. Cool completely in pan on wire rack. When chocolate is set, cut into 2-inch squares.

Makes 16 brownies

*Bittersweet chocolate is available in specialty food stores. One square unsweetened chocolate plus 2 squares semisweet chocolate may be substituted.

HONEY BROWNIES

The rich chocolate taste of these cake-like brownies is enhanced by golden honey.

1 cup (6 ounces) semisweet chocolate chips
6 tablespoons butter or margarine
2 eggs
⅓ cup honey
1 teaspoon vanilla
½ cup all-purpose flour
½ teaspoon baking powder
Dash salt
1 cup chopped walnuts

Preheat oven to 350°F. Butter an 8-inch square pan. Melt chocolate and butter in medium-sized heavy saucepan over low heat. Remove from heat; cool slightly. Stir in eggs, honey and vanilla. Combine flour, baking powder and salt in small bowl. Stir into chocolate mixture with walnuts. Spread batter evenly in prepared pan. Bake 20 to 25 minutes or just until center feels springy. Cool in pan on wire rack. Cut into 2-inch squares.

Makes 16 brownies

Raspberry Fudge Brownies

DECADENT BROWNIES

Designed after the popular dessert called chocolate decadence, these brownies are sinfully rich, smooth and chocolatey.

½ cup dark corn syrup
½ cup butter or margarine
6 squares (1 ounce each) semisweet chocolate
¾ cup sugar
3 eggs
1 cup all-purpose flour
1 cup chopped walnuts
1 teaspoon vanilla
  Fudge Glaze (recipe follows)

Preheat oven to 350°F. Grease an 8-inch square pan. Combine corn syrup, butter and chocolate in large heavy saucepan. Place over low heat; stir until chocolate is melted and ingredients are blended. Remove from heat; blend in sugar. Stir in eggs, flour, chopped walnuts and vanilla. Spread batter evenly in prepared pan. Bake 20 to 25 minutes or just until center is set. Do not overbake. Meanwhile, prepare Fudge Glaze. Remove brownies from oven. Immediately spread glaze evenly over hot brownies. Cool in pan on wire rack. Cut into 2-inch squares.

Makes 16 brownies

FUDGE GLAZE
3 squares (1 ounce each) semisweet chocolate
2 tablespoons dark corn syrup
1 tablespoon butter or margarine
1 teaspoon light cream or milk

Combine chocolate, corn syrup and butter in small heavy saucepan. Stir over low heat until chocolate is melted; mix in cream.

CINNAMON-WHEAT BROWNIES

2 squares (1 ounce each) unsweetened chocolate
½ cup butter or margarine, softened
1 cup packed dark brown sugar
2 eggs
1 teaspoon ground cinnamon
1 teaspoon vanilla
¼ teaspoon baking powder
¼ teaspoon ground ginger
⅛ teaspoon ground cloves
½ cup whole wheat flour
1 cup coarsely chopped walnuts

Preheat oven to 350°F. Butter an 8-inch square pan. Melt chocolate in top of double boiler over hot, not boiling, water. Remove from heat; cool. Cream butter, sugar, eggs and melted chocolate in large bowl until light and smooth. Blend in cinnamon, vanilla, baking powder, ginger and cloves. Stir in flour and walnuts until well blended. Spread batter evenly in prepared pan. Bake 25 to 30 minutes or until top feels firm and dry. Do not overbake. Cool in pan on wire rack. Cut into 2-inch squares.

Makes 16 brownies

MISSISSIPPI MUD BARS

½ cup butter or margarine, softened
¾ cup packed brown sugar
1 teaspoon vanilla
1 egg
½ teaspoon baking soda
¼ teaspoon salt
1 cup plus 2 tablespoons all-purpose flour
1 cup (6 ounces) semisweet chocolate chips, divided
1 cup (6 ounces) white chocolate chips, divided
½ cup chopped walnuts or pecans

Preheat oven to 375°F. Line a 9-inch square pan with foil; grease the foil. Cream butter and sugar in large bowl until blended and smooth. Beat in vanilla and egg until light. Blend in baking soda and salt. Add flour, mixing until well blended. Stir in ¾ cup *each* of the semisweet and white chocolate chips and the nuts. Spread dough in prepared pan. Bake 23 to 25 minutes or until center feels firm. Do not overbake. Remove from oven; sprinkle remaining ¼ cup *each* semisweet and white chocolate chips over the top. Let stand a few minutes until chips melt, then spread evenly over bars. Cool in pan on wire rack until chocolate is set. Cut into 2×1-inch bars.

Makes about 3 dozen bars

APPLESAUCE FUDGE BARS

Applesauce and a double dose of chocolate make these moist and fudgy.

3 squares (1 ounce each) semisweet chocolate
½ cup butter or margarine
⅔ cup unsweetened applesauce
2 eggs, beaten
1 cup packed light brown sugar
1 teaspoon vanilla
1 cup all-purpose flour
½ teaspoon baking powder
¼ teaspoon baking soda
½ cup walnuts, chopped
1 cup (6 ounces) milk chocolate chips

Preheat oven to 350°F. Grease a 9-inch square pan. Melt semisweet chocolate and butter in small heavy saucepan over low heat. Remove from heat; cool. Combine applesauce, eggs, sugar and vanilla in large bowl. Combine flour, baking powder and baking soda in small bowl. Mix dry ingredients into applesauce mixture; blend in chocolate mixture. Spread batter evenly in prepared pan. Sprinkle nuts over the top. Bake 25 to 30 minutes or just until set. Remove from oven; sprinkle chocolate chips over the top. Let stand a few minutes until chips melt, then spread evenly over bars. Cool in pan on wire rack. Cut into 2×1-inch bars.

Makes about 3 dozen bars

ROCKY ROAD BROWNIES

½ cup butter or margarine
½ cup unsweetened cocoa
1 cup sugar
1 egg
½ cup all-purpose flour
¼ cup buttermilk
1 teaspoon vanilla
1 cup miniature
    marshmallows
1 cup coarsely chopped
    walnuts
1 cup (6 ounces) semisweet
    chocolate chips

Preheat oven to 350°F. Lightly grease an 8-inch square pan. Combine butter and cocoa in medium-sized heavy saucepan over low heat, stirring constantly until smooth. Remove from heat; stir in sugar, egg, flour, buttermilk and vanilla. Mix until smooth. Spread batter evenly in prepared pan. Bake 25 minutes or until center feels dry. (Do not overbake or brownies will be dry.) Remove from oven; sprinkle marshmallows, walnuts and chocolate chips over the top. Return to oven for 3 to 5 minutes or just until topping is warmed enough to meld together. Cool in pan on wire rack. Cut into 2-inch squares.

Makes 16 brownies

CHUNKY OATMEAL BARS

Large chocolate chunks are scattered throughout these buttery oatmeal bars. If you can't find chocolate chunks, cut chocolate candy bars into chunks.

¾ cup butter or margarine,
    softened
1 cup packed light brown
    sugar
2 teaspoons vanilla
1 cup all-purpose flour
2 tablespoons unsweetened
    cocoa
1½ teaspoons baking powder
¼ teaspoon salt
¼ cup water
2 cups uncooked rolled oats
1 package (12 ounces)
    semisweet chocolate
    chunks

Preheat oven to 375°F. Lightly grease a 9-inch square pan. Cream butter with sugar until smooth. Add vanilla, beating until light. Combine flour, cocoa, baking powder and salt in small bowl. Blend into creamed mixture with water. Stir in oats and chocolate chunks. Spread dough evenly in prepared pan. Bake 25 to 30 minutes or just until center feels firm. Cool in pan on wire rack. Cut into 2×1-inch bars.

Makes about 3 dozen bars

Rocky Road Brownies

DOUBLE CHOCOLATE
CRISPY BARS

Both sides of these crispy bars are painted with chocolate—dark chocolate on one side, white chocolate on the other.

6 cups crispy rice cereal
½ cup peanut butter
⅓ cup butter or margarine
2 squares (1 ounce each) unsweetened chocolate
1 package (8 ounces) marshmallows
1 cup (6 ounces) semisweet chocolate chips *or* 6 ounces bittersweet chocolate, chopped
6 ounces white chocolate, chopped
2 teaspoons shortening, divided

Preheat oven to 350°F. Line a 13×9-inch pan with waxed paper. Spread cereal on cookie sheet; toast in oven 10 minutes or until crispy. Place in large bowl. Meanwhile, combine peanut butter, butter and unsweetened chocolate in large heavy saucepan. Stir over low heat until chocolate is melted. Add marshmallows; stir until melted and smooth. Pour chocolate mixture over cereal; mix until evenly coated. Press firmly into prepared pan. Place semisweet and white chocolates into separate bowls. Add 1 teaspoon shortening to each bowl. Place bowls over very warm water; stir until chocolates are melted. Spread top of bars with melted semisweet chocolate; cool until chocolate is set. Turn bars out of pan onto a sheet of waxed paper, chocolate side down. Remove waxed paper from bottom of bars; spread white chocolate over surface. Cool until chocolate is set. Cut into 2×1½-inch bars using a sharp, thin knife.

Makes about 3 dozen bars

Clockwise from top left: Double Chocolate Crispy Bars, Chocolate Macadamia Bars (page 48), Naomi's Revel Bars (page 48)

CHOCOLATE MACADAMIA BARS

12 squares (1 ounce each)
   bittersweet chocolate *or*
   1 package (12 ounces)
   semisweet chocolate
   chips
1 package (8 ounces) cream
   cheese, softened
⅔ cup whipping cream or
   undiluted evaporated
   milk
1 cup chopped macadamia
   nuts or almonds
1 teaspoon vanilla, divided
1 cup butter or margarine,
   softened
1½ cups sugar
1 egg
3 cups all-purpose flour
1 teaspoon baking powder
¼ teaspoon salt

Preheat oven to 375°F. Lightly grease a 13×9-inch pan. Combine chocolate, cream cheese and cream in large heavy saucepan. Stir over low heat until chocolate is melted and mixture is smooth. Remove from heat; stir in nuts and ½ teaspoon of the vanilla. Cream butter and sugar in large bowl. Beat in egg and remaining ½ teaspoon vanilla. Add flour, baking powder and salt, blending well. Press half of the butter mixture on bottom of prepared pan. Spread chocolate mixture evenly over the top. Sprinkle remaining butter mixture over chocolate. Bake 35 to 40 minutes or until golden brown. Cool in pan on wire rack. Cut into 2×1½-inch bars.

Makes about 3 dozen bars

NAOMI'S REVEL BARS

1 cup plus 2 tablespoons
   butter or margarine,
   softened
2 cups packed brown sugar
2 eggs
2 teaspoons vanilla
2½ cups all-purpose flour
1 teaspoon baking soda
3 cups uncooked rolled oats
1 package (12 ounces)
   semisweet chocolate
   chips
1 can (14 ounces) sweetened
   condensed milk

Preheat oven to 325°F. Lightly grease a 13×9-inch pan. Cream the 1 cup butter and the sugar in large bowl. Add eggs; beat until light. Blend in vanilla. Combine flour and baking soda; stir into creamed mixture. Blend in oats. Spread ¾ of the oat mixture evenly in prepared pan. Combine chocolate chips, milk and the 2 tablespoons butter in small heavy saucepan. Stir over low heat until chocolate is melted. Pour chocolate mixture evenly over mixture in pan. Dot with remaining oat mixture. Bake 20 to 25 minutes or until edges are browned and center feels firm. Cool in pan on wire rack. Cut into 2×1½-inch bars.

Makes about 3 dozen bars

NORMA D's COCOA BROWNIES

This large pan of cake-like brownies is perfect for a potluck supper or club meeting.

2 cups all-purpose flour
2 cups granulated sugar
1 cup butter or margarine
1 cup hot coffee
¼ cup unsweetened cocoa
½ cup buttermilk
2 eggs, slightly beaten
1 teaspoon baking soda
1 teaspoon vanilla
Cocoa Frosting (recipe follows)

Preheat oven to 400°F. Butter a 17½×11-inch jelly-roll pan. Combine flour and granulated sugar in large bowl. Combine butter, coffee and cocoa in small heavy saucepan. Bring to a boil over medium heat, stirring constantly. Combine buttermilk, eggs, baking soda and vanilla in small bowl. Stir cocoa mixture into flour mixture until smooth. Stir in buttermilk mixture until well blended. Pour batter into prepared pan. Bake 20 minutes or until center springs back when touched. Meanwhile, prepare Cocoa Frosting. Remove brownies from oven. Immediately pour warm frosting over hot brownies, spreading evenly. Cool in pan on wire rack. Cut into 2½-inch squares.

Makes about 30 brownies

COCOA FROSTING
½ cup butter or margarine
2 tablespoons unsweetened cocoa
¼ cup milk
3½ cups powdered sugar
1 teaspoon vanilla

Combine butter, cocoa and milk in large saucepan. Bring to a boil over medium heat. Remove from heat. Stir in powdered sugar and vanilla; beat until smooth.

CHOCOLATE CHIP & SOUR CREAM BROWNIES

½ cup butter or margarine, softened
1 cup packed light brown sugar
1 egg
1 cup sour cream
1 teaspoon vanilla
½ cup unsweetened cocoa
½ teaspoon baking soda
¼ teaspoon salt
2 cups all-purpose flour
1 cup (6 ounces) semisweet chocolate chips
Powdered sugar

Preheat oven to 350°F. Butter a 13×9-inch pan. Cream butter and brown sugar in large bowl until blended. Add egg, sour cream and vanilla; beat until light. Add cocoa, baking soda and salt; beat until smooth. Blend in flour until well mixed. Stir in chocolate chips; spread batter evenly in prepared pan. Bake 25 to 30 minutes or until center springs back when touched. Cool in pan on wire rack. Sift powdered sugar over the top. Cut into 2½×1½-inch bars.

Makes about 30 brownies

ALMOND CHEESECAKE BROWNIES

4 squares (1 ounce each)
   semisweet chocolate
5 tablespoons butter or
   margarine, divided
1 package (3 ounces) cream
   cheese, softened
1 cup granulated sugar,
   divided
3 eggs, divided
½ cup plus 1 tablespoon
   all-purpose flour
1½ teaspoons vanilla, divided
½ teaspoon baking powder
¼ teaspoon salt
½ teaspoon almond extract
½ cup chopped or slivered
   almonds
   Almond Icing (recipe
   follows)

Preheat oven to 350°F. Butter an 8-inch square pan. Melt chocolate and 3 tablespoons of the butter in small heavy saucepan over low heat; set aside. Mix cream cheese with remaining 2 tablespoons butter in small bowl. Slowly add ¼ cup of the granulated sugar, blending well. Add 1 egg, the 1 tablespoon flour and ½ teaspoon of the vanilla; set aside. Beat remaining 2 eggs and ¾ cup granulated sugar in large bowl until light. Add the baking powder, salt and ½ cup flour. Blend in chocolate mixture, remaining 1 teaspoon vanilla and the almond extract. Stir in almonds. Spread half of the chocolate mixture in prepared pan. Cover with cream cheese mixture, then spoon remaining chocolate mixture over the top. Swirl with knife or spatula to create a marbled effect. Bake 30 to 35 minutes or until set in center. Do not overbake. Meanwhile, prepare Almond Icing. Cool brownies 5 minutes, then spread icing evenly over the top. Cool completely in pan on wire rack. Cut into 2-inch squares.

Makes 16 brownies

ALMOND ICING
½ cup semisweet chocolate
   chips
2 tablespoons butter or
   margarine
3 tablespoons milk
¼ teaspoon almond extract
1 cup powdered sugar

Combine chocolate chips, butter, milk and almond extract in small heavy saucepan. Stir over low heat until chocolate is melted. Add powdered sugar; beat until glossy and easy to spread.

Clockwise from left: Almond Cheesecake Brownies,
Chocolate Dream Bars (page 52), Chocolate-Mint Brownies (page 53)

CHOCOLATE DREAM BARS

½ cup butter or margarine,
    softened
1½ cups packed light brown
    sugar, divided
1 egg yolk
1 cup plus 2 tablespoons
    all-purpose flour
2 eggs
1 cup (6 ounces) semisweet
    chocolate chips
½ cup chopped toasted
    walnuts

Preheat oven to 375°F. Grease a 13×9-inch pan. Cream butter with ½ cup of the sugar and the egg yolk in large bowl until light and well blended. (There should be no brown sugar lumps.) Stir in the 1 cup flour until well blended. Press dough on bottom of prepared pan. Bake 12 to 15 minutes or until golden. Meanwhile, beat remaining 1 cup sugar, the 2 tablespoons flour and eggs in same bowl until light and frothy. Spread mixture over hot baked crust. Return to oven; bake about 15 minutes or until topping is set. Remove from oven; sprinkle chocolate chips over the top. Let stand a few minutes until chips melt, then spread evenly over bars. Sprinkle walnuts over chocolate. Cool in pan on wire rack. Cut into 2×1-inch bars.

Makes about 5 dozen bars

TEX-MEX BROWNIES

Ground red pepper gives these south-of-the-border brownies a slightly hot bite that goes well with chocolate.

½ cup butter or margarine
2 squares (1 ounce each)
    unsweetened chocolate
½ to 1 teaspoon ground red
    pepper
2 eggs
1 cup sugar
½ cup all-purpose flour
1 teaspoon vanilla
1 cup (6 ounces) semisweet
    chocolate chips

Preheat oven to 325°F. Grease and flour an 8-inch square pan. Melt butter and unsweetened chocolate in small heavy saucepan over low heat. Remove from heat. Stir in pepper; cool. Beat eggs in medium bowl until light. Add sugar, beating well. Blend in chocolate mixture. Stir in flour and vanilla. Spread batter evenly in prepared pan. Bake 30 minutes or until firm in center. Remove from oven; sprinkle chocolate chips over the top. Let stand until chocolate is melted, then spread evenly over brownies. Cool completely in pan on wire rack. Cut into 2-inch squares.

Makes 16 brownies

CHOCOLATE-MINT BROWNIES

½ cup butter or margarine
2 squares (1 ounce each) unsweetened chocolate
2 eggs
1 cup packed light brown sugar
½ cup all-purpose flour
1 teaspoon vanilla
Mint Frosting (recipe follows)
Chocolate Glaze (recipe follows)

Preheat oven to 350°F. Grease and flour an 8-inch square pan. Melt butter and chocolate in small heavy saucepan over low heat; stir to blend. Remove from heat; cool. Beat eggs in medium bowl until light. Add brown sugar, beating well. Blend in chocolate mixture. Stir in flour and vanilla. Spread batter evenly in prepared pan. Bake 30 minutes or until firm in center. Cool in pan on wire rack. Prepare Mint Frosting. Spread over the top; refrigerate until firm. Prepare Chocolate Glaze. Drizzle over frosting; refrigerate until firm. Cut into 2-inch squares.

Makes 16 brownies

MINT FROSTING

1½ cups powdered sugar
2 to 3 tablespoons light cream or milk
1 tablespoon butter or margarine, softened
½ teaspoon peppermint extract
1 to 2 drops green food coloring

Blend powdered sugar, 2 tablespoons cream and the butter in small bowl until smooth. Add more cream, if necessary, to make spreading consistency. Blend in peppermint extract and enough green food coloring to make a pale mint-green color.

CHOCOLATE GLAZE

½ cup semisweet chocolate chips
2 tablespoons butter or margarine

Place chocolate chips and butter in small bowl over hot water. Stir until melted and smooth.

MARBLED PEANUT-BUTTER BROWNIES

Swirls of peanut butter and chocolate form an unbeatable flavor combination.

½ cup butter or margarine, softened
¼ cup peanut butter
1 cup packed light brown sugar
½ cup granulated sugar
3 eggs
1 teaspoon vanilla
2 cups all-purpose flour
2 teaspoons baking powder
⅛ teaspoon salt
1 cup chocolate-flavored syrup
½ cup coarsely chopped salted mixed nuts

Preheat oven to 350°F. Lightly grease a 13×9-inch pan. Cream butter and peanut butter in large bowl until blended; stir in sugars. Beat in eggs, one at a time, until batter is light. Blend in vanilla. Combine flour, baking powder and salt in small bowl. Stir into creamed mixture. Spread half of the batter evenly in prepared pan. Spread syrup over the top. Spoon remaining batter over syrup. Swirl with knife or spatula to create a marbled effect. Sprinkle chopped nuts over the top. Bake 35 to 40 minutes or until lightly browned. Cool in pan on wire rack. Cut into 2-inch squares.

Makes about 2 dozen brownies

WEST HAVEN DATE BARS

1 cup boiling water
1 cup chopped pitted dates
½ cup butter or margarine, softened
1 cup sugar
2 eggs
1 teaspoon vanilla
1½ cups all-purpose flour
2 tablespoons unsweetened cocoa
1 teaspoon baking soda
1 cup (6 ounces) semisweet chocolate chips
½ cup chopped walnuts or pecans

Preheat oven to 350°F. Lightly grease a 13×9-inch pan. Pour boiling water over dates in small bowl; let stand until cooled. Cream butter with sugar in large bowl. Add eggs and vanilla; beat until light. Blend in flour, cocoa and baking soda to make a smooth dough. Stir in date mixture. Spread batter evenly in prepared pan. Sprinkle chocolate chips and nuts over the top. Bake 25 to 30 minutes or just until center feels firm. Cut into 2×1½-inch bars while still warm.

Makes about 3 dozen bars

Marbled Peanut-Butter Brownies

MOCHA FUDGE BROWNIES

3 squares (1 ounce each) semisweet chocolate
½ cup butter or margarine, softened
¾ cup sugar
2 eggs
2 teaspoons instant espresso coffee powder
1 teaspoon vanilla
½ cup all-purpose flour
½ cup chopped toasted almonds
1 cup (6 ounces) milk chocolate chips, divided

Preheat oven to 350°F. Butter an 8-inch square pan. Melt semisweet chocolate in top of double boiler over hot, not boiling, water. Remove from heat; cool. Cream butter and sugar in medium bowl. Beat in eggs until light and fluffy. Add melted chocolate, coffee powder and vanilla. Blend in flour, almonds and ½ cup of the chocolate chips. Spread batter evenly in prepared pan. Bake 25 minutes or just until firm in center. Remove from oven; sprinkle remaining ½ cup chocolate chips over the top. Let stand a few minutes until chips melt, then spread evenly over brownies. Cool completely in pan on wire rack. Cut into 2-inch squares.

Makes 16 brownies

CHOCOLATE CARAMEL BARS

2 cups all-purpose flour
1½ cups packed brown sugar, divided
1¼ cups butter or margarine, softened, divided
1 cup chopped pecans
1 cup (6 ounces) milk chocolate chips

Preheat oven to 350°F. Blend flour with 1 cup of the sugar and ½ cup of the butter in large bowl until crumbly. Press firmly on bottom of a 13×9-inch pan; sprinkle pecans evenly over the top. Combine remaining ½ cup sugar and ¾ cup butter in small saucepan. Cook over medium heat, stirring constantly, until mixture comes to a boil. Boil 1 minute, stirring constantly, until butter and sugar blend into a caramel sauce. Pour sauce evenly over pecans in pan. Bake 18 to 20 minutes or until caramel layer bubbles evenly all over. Remove from oven; sprinkle chocolate chips over the top. Let stand a few minutes until chips melt, then spread evenly over bars. Cool until chocolate is set, then cut into 2×1-inch bars.

Makes about 5 dozen bars

TOFFEE BARS

The crisp, brown-sugar base of these milk-chocolate-topped treats will remind you of a favorite candy bar.

½ cup butter or margarine, softened
½ cup packed light brown sugar
1 egg yolk
1 teaspoon vanilla
1 cup all-purpose flour
1 cup (6 ounces) milk chocolate chips
½ cup chopped walnuts or pecans

Preheat oven to 350°F. Lightly grease a 13×9-inch pan. Cream butter and sugar in large bowl. Blend in egg yolk and vanilla. Stir in flour until well blended. Press on bottom of prepared pan. Bake 15 minutes or until golden. Remove from oven; sprinkle chocolate chips over the top. Let stand a few minutes until chips melt, then spread evenly over bars. Sprinkle nuts over chocolate. Score into 2×1½-inch bars while still warm. Cool completely in pan on wire rack before cutting and removing from pan.

Makes about 3 dozen bars

FRUIT & PECAN BROWNIES

2 squares (1 ounce each) unsweetened chocolate
½ cup butter or margarine, softened
1 cup sugar
2 eggs
1 teaspoon vanilla
½ cup all-purpose flour
1 cup chopped dried mixed fruit
1 cup coarsely chopped pecans, divided
1 cup (6 ounces) semisweet chocolate chips, divided

Preheat oven to 350°F. Butter an 8-inch square pan. Melt unsweetened chocolate in top of double boiler over hot, not boiling, water. Remove from heat; cool. Cream butter and sugar in large bowl until smooth. Mix in eggs, beating until light and fluffy. Blend in melted chocolate and vanilla. Stir in flour, fruit, ½ cup of the pecans and ½ cup of the chocolate chips. Spread batter evenly in prepared pan. Sprinkle remaining ½ cup pecans and ½ cup chocolate chips over the top. Bake 25 to 30 minutes or just until center feels firm. Do not overbake. Remove from oven; cover while still warm with waxed paper or foil. Cool completely in pan on wire rack. Cut into 2-inch squares.

Makes 16 brownies

Chocolate Chippers

Clockwise from top right: White Chocolate and Cocoa Chippers (page 62), Aloha Chippers (page 62), Peanutty Double Chip Cookies (page 63)

CHOCOLATE CHIP
CINNAMON CRINKLES

Rolling the dough in cinnamon sugar makes these cookies crinkly on top.

½ cup butter or margarine,
  softened
½ cup packed brown sugar
¼ cup plus 2 tablespoons
  granulated sugar
1 tcaspoon vanilla
1 egg
1 teaspoon cream of tartar
½ teaspoon baking soda
⅛ teaspoon salt
1⅓ cups all-purpose flour
1 cup (6 ounces) semisweet
  chocolate chips
2 teaspoons unsweetened
  cocoa
1 teaspoon ground
  cinnamon

Preheat oven to 400°F. Line cookie sheets with parchment paper or leave ungreased. Cream butter with brown sugar, the ¼ cup granulated sugar, vanilla and egg in large bowl until light and fluffy. Beat in cream of tartar, baking soda and salt. Add flour; mix until dough is blended and stiff. Stir in chocolate chips. Combine the 2 tablespoons granulated sugar, the cocoa and cinnamon in small bowl. Shape rounded teaspoonfuls of dough into balls about 1¼ inches in diameter. Roll balls in cinnamon mixture until coated on all sides. Place 2 inches apart on cookie sheets. Bake 8 to 10 minutes or until firm. Do not overbake. Remove to wire racks to cool.

Makes about 3½ dozen cookies

CHOCOLATE CHIP
WAFER COOKIES

The trick to handling these delicate cookies is to line the cookie sheets with greased foil. When the cookies are cool, it's easy to peel the foil right off them.

½ cup butter or margarine,
  softened
½ cup sugar
1 egg
1 teaspoon vanilla
½ cup all-purpose flour
  Dash salt
1 cup (6 ounces) semisweet
  chocolate chips
⅓ cup chopped pecans or
  walnuts

Preheat oven to 350°F. Line cookie sheets with foil; lightly grease foil. Cream butter and sugar in large bowl until light. Add egg; beat until creamy. Stir in vanilla, flour and salt. Add chocolate chips and nuts; mix until well blended. Drop dough by teaspoonfuls 3 inches apart onto prepared cookie sheets. Bake 7 to 10 minutes or until edges are golden and centers are set. (Cookies are soft when hot, but become crispy as they cool.) Cool completely on foil, then peel foil from cookies.

Makes about 2 dozen cookies

*Top to bottom: Mrs. J's Chip Cookies (page 63), Chocolate Chip
Wafer Cookies, Chocolate Chip Cinnamon Crinkles*

ALOHA CHIPPERS

½ cup butter or margarine, softened
⅓ cup granulated sugar
⅓ cup packed light brown sugar
1 egg
1 tablespoon dark rum or water
1 teaspoon vanilla
½ teaspoon baking soda
⅛ teaspoon salt
1¼ cups all-purpose flour
½ cup semisweet chocolate chips
1 cup (6 ounces) white chocolate chips
½ cup flaked coconut
½ cup coarsely chopped macadamia nuts
Flaked coconut

Preheat oven to 375°F. Line cookie sheets with parchment paper or leave ungreased. Cream butter, sugars, egg, rum, vanilla, baking soda and salt in large bowl until light and fluffy. Blend in flour until dough is smooth and stiff. Stir in semisweet and white chocolate chips, ½ cup coconut and the macadamia nuts. Drop dough by teaspoonfuls 2 inches apart onto cookie sheets. Sprinkle tops of cookies with additional coconut. Bake 8 to 10 minutes or until just firm in center. Do not overbake. Remove to wire racks to cool.

Makes about 3 dozen cookies

WHITE CHOCOLATE & COCOA CHIPPERS

¾ cup butter or margarine, softened
½ cup granulated sugar
½ cup packed brown sugar
1 egg
2 tablespoons water
½ cup unsweetened cocoa
¾ teaspoon baking soda
½ teaspoon vanilla
¼ teaspoon salt
1⅓ cups all-purpose flour
1½ cups (10 to 12 ounces) large white chocolate chips
1 cup coarsely chopped pecans or walnuts

Preheat oven to 375°F. Line cookie sheets with parchment paper or leave ungreased. Cream butter, sugars, egg and water in large bowl until light and fluffy. Blend in cocoa, baking soda, vanilla and salt. Blend in flour until well mixed. Stir in white chocolate chips and nuts. Drop dough by rounded tablespoonfuls 3 inches apart onto cookie sheets. Bake 8 to 10 minutes or until firm in center. Do not overbake. Remove to wire racks to cool.

Makes about 4 dozen cookies

PEANUTTY DOUBLE CHIP COOKIES

½ cup butter or margarine, softened
¾ cup packed light brown sugar
¾ cup granulated sugar
2 eggs
1 teaspoon baking soda
1 teaspoon vanilla
2 cups all-purpose flour
1 cup chunky peanut butter
1 cup (6 ounces) semisweet or milk chocolate chips
1 cup (6 ounces) peanut butter chips

Preheat oven to 350°F. Lightly grease cookie sheets or line with parchment paper. Cream butter and sugars in large bowl until blended. Add eggs, baking soda and vanilla; beat until light. Blend in flour and peanut butter until dough is stiff and smooth. Stir in chocolate and peanut butter chips. Drop dough by teaspoonfuls 2 inches apart onto prepared cookie sheets. Press cookies down with tines of fork to flatten slightly. Bake 12 minutes or until just barely done. Do not overbake. Remove to wire racks to cool.

Makes about 5 dozen cookies

MRS. J'S CHIP COOKIES

Crispy rice cereal, pulverized into a flour, adds flavor and texture to these cookies.

4 cups crispy rice cereal
1 milk chocolate crunch bar (5 ounces), broken into squares
2 cups all-purpose flour
1 teaspoon baking powder
1 teaspoon baking soda
¼ teaspoon salt
1 cup butter or margarine, softened
1 cup granulated sugar
1 cup packed light brown sugar
2 eggs
1 teaspoon vanilla
1 package (12 ounces) semisweet chocolate chips
1½ cups chopped walnuts

Preheat oven to 375°F. Line cookie sheets with parchment paper or leave ungreased. Process cereal in blender or food processor until pulverized. Add chocolate bar; continue processing until both chocolate and cereal are completely ground. Add flour, baking powder, baking soda and salt; process until blended. Cream butter and sugars in large bowl. Add eggs; beat until light. Blend in vanilla. Add flour mixture; blend until smooth. Stir in chocolate chips and walnuts until blended. Shape dough into walnut-sized balls. Place 2 inches apart on cookie sheets. Bake 10 to 12 minutes or until firm in center. Do not overbake. Remove to wire racks to cool.

Makes about 8 dozen cookies

DOUBLE CHOCOLATE CHUNK COOKIES

2 squares (1 ounce each)
    unsweetened chocolate
3 eggs
1 cup vegetable oil
¾ cup packed brown sugar
1 teaspoon baking powder
1 teaspoon vanilla
¼ teaspoon baking soda
¼ teaspoon salt
2⅓ cups all-purpose flour
1 package (12 ounces)
    semisweet chocolate
    chunks

Preheat oven to 350°F. Lightly grease cookie sheets or line with parchment paper. Melt unsweetened chocolate in top of double boiler over hot, not boiling, water. Remove from heat; cool. Beat eggs in large bowl until foamy. Add the oil and sugar; continue beating until light and frothy. Blend in baking powder, vanilla, baking soda, salt and melted chocolate. Mix in flour until smooth. Stir in chocolate chunks. Shape dough into walnut-sized balls. Place 2 inches apart on prepared cookie sheets. Bake 10 to 12 minutes or until firm in center. Do not overbake. Remove to wire racks to cool.

Makes about 4½ dozen cookies

White Chocolate Chunk Cookies:
Substitute one package (12 ounces) white chocolate chunks *or* two white chocolate candy bars (5 to 6 ounces each), cut into chunks, for the semisweet chocolate chunks.

CHOCOLATE CHUNK COOKIES

3 eggs
1 cup vegetable oil
¾ cup packed brown sugar
1 teaspoon baking powder
1 teaspoon vanilla
¼ teaspoon baking soda
¼ teaspoon salt
2½ cups all-purpose flour
1 package (12 ounces)
    semisweet chocolate
    chunks

Preheat oven to 350°F. Lightly grease cookie sheets or line with parchment paper. Beat eggs in large bowl until foamy. Add oil and sugar; beating until light and frothy. Blend in baking powder, vanilla, baking soda and salt. Mix in flour until dough is smooth. Stir in chocolate chunks. Shape dough into walnut-sized balls. Place 2 inches apart on prepared cookie sheets. Bake 10 to 12 minutes or until lightly browned. Remove to wire racks to cool.

Makes about 4½ dozen cookies

White Chocolate Chunk Cookies

CINNAMON-MOCHA CHIP COOKIES

1 cup butter or margarine, softened
1 cup packed light brown sugar
1 tablespoon instant espresso coffee powder
1 tablespoon boiling water
1 teaspoon vanilla
1 egg
2 cups all-purpose flour
1 teaspoon baking soda
1 teaspoon ground cinnamon
¼ teaspoon salt
1 package (12 ounces) milk chocolate chips
1½ cups coarsely chopped walnuts

Preheat oven to 375°F. Line cookie sheets with parchment paper or leave ungreased. Cream butter and sugar in large bowl until smooth. Dissolve coffee powder in water. Add to creamed mixture with vanilla and egg; beat until light. Combine flour, baking soda, cinnamon and salt in small bowl. Blend into creamed mixture until smooth. Stir in chocolate chips and walnuts. Drop dough by rounded tablespoonfuls 3 inches apart onto cookie sheets. Bake 7 to 9 minutes or until just firm in center. Cool 3 minutes on cookie sheet, then remove to wire racks to cool completely.

Makes about 3 dozen cookies

ULTIMATE WHITE & DARK CHOCOLATE CHIPPERS

1 cup butter or margarine, softened
¾ cup granulated sugar
¾ cup packed light brown sugar
2 eggs
2 tablespoons almond-flavored liqueur or water
1 teaspoon baking soda
1 teaspoon vanilla
¼ teaspoon salt
2⅓ cups all-purpose flour
1 cup (6 ounces) semisweet chocolate chips
1 cup (6 ounces) white chocolate chips
1 cup coarsely chopped pecans

Preheat oven to 375°F. Line cookie sheets with parchment paper or leave ungreased. Cream butter, sugars, eggs, liqueur, baking soda, vanilla and salt in large bowl until light and fluffy. Blend in flour until dough is smooth and stiff. Stir in semisweet and white chocolate chips and pecans. Drop dough by teaspoonfuls 2 inches apart onto prepared cookie sheets. Bake 8 to 10 minutes or until just firm in center. Do not overbake. Remove to wire racks to cool.

Makes about 5 dozen cookies

PISTACHIO CHIP COOKIES

Serve these cookies for dessert as an elegant accompaniment to ice cream. Be sure to follow the instructions and bake them on greased foil.

½ cup butter or margarine
⅓ cup light corn syrup
2 tablespoons frozen orange juice concentrate, thawed
1 tablespoon grated orange zest
⅔ cup packed dark brown sugar
1 cup all-purpose flour
½ cup chopped pistachio nuts
1 cup (6 ounces) semisweet chocolate chips

Preheat oven to 375°F. Line cookie sheets with foil; lightly grease foil. Combine butter, corn syrup, orange concentrate, orange zest and sugar in medium saucepan. Bring to a boil over medium heat, stirring constantly. Remove from heat; gradually stir in flour and nuts. Cool completely. Stir in chocolate chips. Drop batter by teaspoonfuls 3 inches apart onto prepared cookie sheets. Bake 8 to 10 minutes or until golden and lacy. (Cookies are soft when hot, but become crispy as they cool.) Cool completely on foil, then peel foil from cookies.

Makes about 4 dozen cookies

OAT BRAN CHIP COOKIES

Oat bran, touted as a health food, adds a wonderful nutty flavor to cookies.

1 cup oat bran*
2 cups all-purpose flour
½ teaspoon baking soda
1 cup butter or margarine, softened
⅔ cup packed light brown sugar
½ cup granulated sugar
2 eggs
1 teaspoon vanilla
1 package (12 ounces) semisweet chocolate chips

Preheat oven to 350°F. Lightly grease baking sheets or line with parchment paper. Combine oat bran, flour and baking soda in small bowl. Cream butter with sugars, eggs and vanilla in large bowl. Blend in flour mixture; stir in chocolate chips. Drop dough by rounded teaspoonfuls 2 inches apart onto prepared cookie sheets. Bake 13 to 15 minutes or until lightly browned. Remove to wire racks to cool.

Makes about 6½ dozen cookies

*If oat bran has a coarse texture, process it in a blender or food processor until pulverized.

WHOLE GRAIN CHIPPERS

Whole wheat flour, rolled oats and sunflower seeds add nutrients, crunch and flavor to after-school cookies.

1 cup butter or margarine, softened
⅔ cup granulated sugar
1 cup packed light brown sugar
2 eggs
1 teaspoon baking soda
1 teaspoon vanilla
 Pinch salt
1 cup whole wheat flour
1 cup all-purpose flour
2 cups uncooked rolled oats
1 package (12 ounces) semisweet chocolate chips
1 cup sunflower seeds

Preheat oven to 375°F. Lightly grease cookie sheets or line with parchment paper. Cream butter with sugars and eggs in large bowl until light and fluffy. Beat in baking soda, vanilla and salt. Blend in flours and oats to make a stiff dough. Stir in chocolate chips. Shape rounded teaspoonfuls of dough into balls; roll in sunflower seeds. Place 2 inches apart on prepared cookie sheets. Bake 8 to 10 minutes or until firm. Do not overbake. Cool a few minutes on cookie sheet, then remove to wire racks to cool completely.

Makes about 6 dozen cookies

WHITE CHOCOLATE CHIP & MACADAMIA COOKIES

Bake these for someone special. Macadamia nuts give them a sensational crunch.

2 squares (1 ounce each) unsweetened chocolate
½ cup butter or margarine, softened
1 cup packed light brown sugar
1 egg
1 teaspoon vanilla
1¼ cups all-purpose flour
½ teaspoon baking soda
1 cup (6 ounces) white chocolate chips
¾ cup macadamia nuts, chopped

Preheat oven to 350°F. Lightly grease cookie sheets or line with parchment paper. Melt unsweetened chocolate in top of double boiler over hot, not boiling, water. Remove from heat; cool. Cream butter, melted chocolate and sugar in large bowl until blended. Add egg and vanilla; beat until light. Blend in flour, baking soda, chocolate chips and macadamia nuts. Drop dough by rounded teaspoonfuls 2 inches apart onto prepared cookie sheets. Bake 10 to 12 minutes or until firm. Do not overbake. Remove to wire racks to cool.

Makes about 4 dozen cookies

Whole Grain Chippers

Special-Day Cookies

Top left to bottom right: Mocha Pecan Pinwheels (page 72), Chocolate Pistachio Fingers (page 84), Chocolate Cherry Cookies (page 73), Orange & Chocolate Ribbon Cookies (page 77), Chocolate Spritz (page 88)

MOCHA PECAN PINWHEELS

1 square (1 ounce)
  unsweetened chocolate
½ cup (1 stick) butter or
  margarine, softened
¾ cup packed brown sugar
1 egg
1 teaspoon vanilla
¼ teaspoon baking soda
1¾ cups all-purpose flour
½ cup chopped pecans
1 teaspoon instant espresso
  coffee powder

Melt chocolate in small bowl over hot water. Stir until smooth. Cream butter, sugar, egg, vanilla and baking soda in large bowl, blending well. Stir in flour to make a stiff dough. Remove half of the dough; place in another bowl. Blend pecans and coffee powder into half of the dough. Stir melted chocolate into remaining dough. Cover doughs; refrigerate 30 minutes. Roll out light-colored dough to a 15×8-inch rectangle between 2 sheets of plastic wrap. Roll chocolate dough out to same dimensions between 2 more sheets of plastic wrap. Remove top sheets of plastic. Place light-colored dough on top of chocolate dough. Roll up firmly, jelly-roll fashion, starting with a long side. Wrap in plastic; freeze. (Dough can be frozen up to 6 weeks.) Preheat oven to 350°F. Line cookie sheets with parchment paper or leave ungreased. Cut frozen dough into ¼-inch-thick slices; place 2 inches apart on cookie sheets. Bake 9 to 12 minutes or until set. Remove to wire racks to cool.

Makes about 5 dozen cookies

CHOCOLATE-COCONUT MACAROONS

4 egg whites
1 teaspoon vanilla
  Dash salt
1½ cups sugar
2⅔ cups flaked coconut
2 tablespoons ground
  chocolate with sugar
  added*

*This type of ground chocolate is available in specialty food stores.

Preheat oven to 325°F. Line cookie sheets with parchment paper or lightly grease and dust with flour. In large clean, dry bowl, beat egg whites with vanilla and salt until stiff, but not dry. Beat in sugar, one tablespoon at a time, until mixture becomes stiff and glossy. Gently fold in coconut and ground chocolate until blended. Drop by rounded teaspoonfuls 2 inches apart onto prepared cookie sheets. Bake 20 minutes or until firm. Remove to wire racks to cool. Store in airtight containers.

Makes about 6 dozen cookies

CHOCOLATE CHERRY COOKIES

2 squares (1 ounce each) unsweetened chocolate
½ cup butter or margarine, softened
½ cup sugar
1 egg
2 cups cake flour
1 teaspoon vanilla
¼ teaspoon salt
Maraschino cherries, well drained (about 48)
1 cup (6 ounces) semisweet or milk chocolate chips

Melt unsweetened chocolate in top of double boiler over hot, not boiling, water. Remove from heat; cool. Cream butter and sugar in large bowl until light. Add egg and melted chocolate; beat until fluffy. Stir in cake flour, vanilla and salt until well blended. Cover; refrigerate until firm, about 1 hour.

Preheat oven to 400°F. Lightly grease cookie sheets or line with parchment paper. Shape dough into 1-inch balls. Place 2 inches apart on prepared cookie sheets. With knuckle of a finger, make a deep indentation in center of each ball. Place a cherry into each indentation. Bake 8 minutes or just until set. Meanwhile, melt chocolate chips in small bowl over hot water. Stir until melted. Remove cookies to wire racks. Drizzle melted chocolate over tops while still warm. Refrigerate until chocolate is set.

Makes about 4 dozen cookies

FUDGE KISSES

Flavored with coconut, nuts and swirls of chocolate, these meringue-based cookies are called kisses—maybe because they crumble when you bite into them.

1 cup (6 ounces) semisweet chocolate chips
2 egg whites
Dash salt
½ teaspoon cider vinegar
½ teaspoon vanilla
½ cup sugar
½ cup flaked coconut
¼ cup chopped walnuts or pecans

Preheat oven to 350°F. Line cookie sheets with parchment paper or lightly grease and sprinkle with flour. Melt chocolate chips in top of double boiler over hot, not boiling, water. Remove from heat; cool. In large clean, dry bowl, beat egg whites with salt until frothy. Beat in vinegar and vanilla. Beat in sugar, one tablespoon at a time, until mixture becomes stiff and glossy. Gently fold in coconut, nuts and melted chocolate until mixture is marbled. Drop mixture by rounded teaspoonfuls 2 inches apart onto prepared cookie sheets. Bake 12 to 15 minutes or until dry on top. Cool completely on cookie sheets. Store in airtight containers.

Makes 3 dozen cookies

RASPBERRY-FILLED CHOCOLATE RAVIOLI

Squares of rich chocolate dough encase a surprise filling of raspberry jam.

2 squares (1 ounce each) bittersweet or semisweet chocolate
1 cup butter or margarine, softened
½ cup granulated sugar
1 egg
1 teaspoon vanilla
½ teaspoon chocolate extract
¼ teaspoon baking soda
Dash salt
2½ cups all-purpose flour
1 to 1¼ cups seedless raspberry jam
Powdered sugar

Melt chocolate in top of double boiler over hot, not boiling, water. Remove from heat; cool. Cream butter and granulated sugar in large bowl until blended. Add egg, vanilla, chocolate extract, baking soda, salt and melted chocolate; beat until light. Blend in flour to make a stiff dough. Divide dough in half. Cover; refrigerate until firm.

Preheat oven to 350°F. Lightly grease cookie sheets or line with parchment paper. Roll out dough, half at a time, ⅛ inch thick between 2 sheets of plastic wrap. Remove top sheet of plastic. (If dough gets too soft and sticks to plastic, refrigerate until firm.) Cut dough into 1½-inch squares. Place half of the squares 2 inches apart on prepared cookie sheets. Place about ½ teaspoon jam in center of each square; top with another square. Using fork, press edges of squares together to seal, then pierce center of each square. Bake 10 minutes or just until edges are browned. Remove to wire racks to cool. Dust lightly with powdered sugar.

Makes about 6 dozen cookies

Raspberry-Filled Chocolate Ravioli

ORANGE & CHOCOLATE RIBBON COOKIES

Use an empty 12×2×2-inch food wrap box to shape these cookies as they chill. A foil, plastic wrap, or waxed paper box is ideal.

1 cup butter or margarine, softened
½ cup sugar
3 egg yolks
2 teaspoons grated orange zest
1 teaspoon orange extract
2¼ cups all-purpose flour, divided
3 tablespoons unsweetened cocoa
1 teaspoon vanilla
1 teaspoon chocolate extract

Cream butter, sugar and egg yolks in large bowl until light and fluffy. Remove half of the mixture; place in another bowl. Add orange zest, orange extract and 1¼ cups of the flour to one half of the mixture; mix until blended and smooth. Shape into a ball. Add cocoa, vanilla and chocolate extract to second half of the mixture; beat until smooth. Stir in remaining 1 cup flour; mix until blended and smooth. Shape into a ball. Cover doughs; refrigerate 10 minutes.

Empty a 12×2×2-inch food wrap box, such as foil or plastic wrap; set aside. Roll out each dough separately on lightly floured surface to a 12×4-inch rectangle. Pat edges of dough to straighten; use rolling pin to level off thickness. Place one of the doughs on top of the other. Using a sharp knife, make a lengthwise cut through center of doughs. Lift half of the dough onto the other to make a long, 4-layer strip of dough. With hands, press dough strips together. Wrap in plastic wrap; fit into food wrap box, pressing down at the top. Close box; refrigerate at least 1 hour or up to 3 days. (For longer storage, freeze up to 6 weeks.)

Preheat oven to 350°F. Lightly grease cookie sheets or line with parchment paper. Cut dough crosswise into ¼-inch-thick slices; place 2 inches apart on prepared cookie sheets. Bake 10 to 12 minutes or until very lightly browned. Remove to wire racks to cool.

Makes about 5 dozen cookies

Orange & Chocolate Ribbon Cookies, Chocolate-Mint Sandwiches (page 78), Cinnamon-Chocolate Cutouts (page 79)

CHOCOLATE-MINT SANDWICHES

2 squares (1 ounce each)
    unsweetened chocolate
½ cup butter or margarine,
    softened
1 cup packed light brown
    sugar
1 teaspoon vanilla
1 egg
⅛ teaspoon baking soda
2 cups all-purpose flour
    Creamy Mint Filling
    (recipe follows)

Melt chocolate in top of double boiler over hot, not boiling, water. Remove from heat; cool. Cream butter and brown sugar in large bowl. Beat in vanilla, egg, melted chocolate and baking soda until light and fluffy. Stir in flour to make a stiff dough. Divide dough into 4 parts. Shape each part into a roll, about 1½ inches in diameter. Wrap in plastic wrap; refrigerate at least 1 hour or up to 2 weeks. (For longer storage, freeze up to 6 weeks.)

Preheat oven to 375°F. Line cookie sheets with parchment paper or leave ungreased. Cut rolls into ⅛-inch-thick slices; place 2 inches apart on cookie sheets. Bake 6 to 7 minutes or until firm. Remove to wire racks to cool. Prepare Creamy Mint Filling. Spread filling on bottoms of half the cookies. Top with remaining cookies, bottom sides down, forming sandwiches.

Makes about 3 dozen sandwich cookies

CREAMY MINT FILLING
2 tablespoons butter or
    margarine, softened
1½ cups powdered sugar
3 to 4 tablespoons light
    cream or half-and-half
¼ teaspoon peppermint
    extract
    Few drops green food
    coloring

Cream butter with powdered sugar and cream in small bowl until smooth and blended. Stir in peppermint extract and food coloring, blending well.

CINNAMON-CHOCOLATE CUTOUTS

2 squares (1 ounce each)
   unsweetened chocolate
½ cup butter or margarine,
   softened
1 cup granulated sugar
1 egg
1 teaspoon vanilla
3 cups all-purpose flour
2 teaspoons ground
   cinnamon
½ teaspoon baking soda
¼ teaspoon salt
½ cup sour cream
   Decorator Icing (recipe
   follows)

Melt chocolate in top of double boiler over hot, not boiling, water. Remove from heat; cool. Cream butter, melted chocolate, granulated sugar, egg and vanilla in large bowl until light. Combine flour, cinnamon, baking soda and salt in small bowl. Stir into creamed mixture with sour cream until smooth. Cover; refrigerate at least 30 minutes.

Preheat oven to 400°F. Lightly grease cookie sheets or line with parchment paper. Roll out dough, one fourth at a time, ¼ inch thick on lightly floured surface. Cut out with cookie cutters. Place 2 inches apart on prepared cookie sheets. Bake 10 minutes or until lightly browned, but not dark. Remove to wire racks to cool. Prepare Decorator Icing. Spoon into pastry bag fitted with small tip or small heavy-duty plastic bag. (If using plastic bag, close securely. With scissors, snip off small corner from one side of bag.) Decorate cookies with icing.

Makes about 6 dozen cookies

DECORATOR ICING
1 egg white*
3½ cups powdered sugar
1 teaspoon almond or
   lemon extract
2 to 3 tablespoons water

Beat egg white in large bowl until frothy. Gradually beat in powdered sugar until blended. Add almond extract and enough water to moisten. Beat until smooth and glossy.

*Use clean, uncracked egg.

SPUMONI BARS

These pretty tri-colored cookies will remind you of the popular Italian ice cream.

¾ cup butter or margarine,
    softened
⅔ cup sugar
3 egg yolks
1 teaspoon vanilla
¼ teaspoon baking powder
⅛ teaspoon salt
2 cups all-purpose flour
12 maraschino cherries, well
    drained and chopped
¼ cup chopped walnuts
¼ cup mint-flavored or plain
    semisweet chocolate
    chips
2 teaspoons water, divided

Preheat oven to 350°F. Cream butter and sugar in large bowl until blended. Beat in egg yolks, vanilla, baking powder and salt until light. Stir in flour to make a stiff dough. Divide dough into 3 equal parts; place each part in small bowl. Add cherries and walnuts to one part, blending well. Melt chocolate chips in small bowl over hot water. Stir until smooth. Add melted chocolate and 1 teaspoon of the water to second part, blending well. Stir remaining 1 teaspoon water into third part. (If doughs are soft, refrigerate 10 minutes.)

Divide each color dough into 4 equal parts. Shape each part into a 6-inch rope by rolling on lightly floured surface. Place one rope of each color side by side on ungreased cookie sheet. Flatten ropes so they attach together making 1 strip of 3 colors. With rolling pin, roll strip directly on cookie sheet until it measures 12×3 inches. With straight edge of knife, score strip crosswise at 1-inch intervals. Repeat with remaining ropes to make a total of 4 tri-colored strips of dough. Bake 12 to 13 minutes or until set but not completely browned; remove from oven. While cookies are still warm, trim lengthwise edges to make them even and cut into individual cookies along score marks. (Cookies will bake together but are easy to cut apart while still warm.) Cool on cookie sheets.

Makes 4 dozen cookies

Spumoni Bars, Chocolate Pistachio Fingers (page 84),
Chocolate-Dipped Oat Cookies (page 84)

DOUBLE-DIPPED
HAZELNUT CRISPS

¾ cup semisweet chocolate
   chips
1 ¼ cups all-purpose flour
¾ cup powdered sugar
⅔ cup whole hazelnuts,
   toasted, hulled and
   pulverized*
¼ teaspoon instant espresso
   coffee powder
   Dash salt
½ cup butter or margarine,
   softened
2 teaspoons vanilla
4 squares (1 ounce each)
   bittersweet or semisweet
   chocolate
4 ounces white chocolate
2 teaspoons shortening,
   divided

Preheat oven to 350°F. Lightly grease cookie sheets or line with parchment paper. Melt chocolate chips in top of double boiler over hot, not boiling, water. Remove from heat; cool. Blend flour, sugar, hazelnuts, coffee powder and salt in large bowl. Blend in butter, melted chocolate and vanilla until dough is stiff but smooth. (If dough is too soft to handle, cover and refrigerate until firm.) Roll out dough, one fourth at a time, ⅛ inch thick on lightly floured surface. Cut out with 2-inch scalloped round cutters. Place 2 inches apart on prepared cookie sheets. Bake 8 minutes or until not quite firm. (Cookies should not brown. They will puff up during baking and then fall again.) Remove to wire racks to cool.

Place bittersweet and white chocolates into separate small bowls. Add 1 teaspoon shortening to each bowl. Place bowls over hot water; stir until chocolate is melted and smooth. Dip cookies, one at a time, halfway into bittersweet chocolate. Place on waxed paper; refrigerate until chocolate is set. Dip other halves of cookies into white chocolate; refrigerate until set. Store cookies in airtight container in cool place. (If cookies are frozen, chocolate may discolor.)

Makes about 4 dozen cookies

*To pulverize hazelnuts, place in food processor or blender. Process until thoroughly ground with a dry, not pasty, texture.

Left to right: Double-Dipped Hazelnut Crisps, Pecan Florentines (page 85)

CHOCOLATE-DIPPED OAT COOKIES

2 cups uncooked rolled oats
¾ cup packed brown sugar
½ cup vegetable oil
½ cup finely chopped walnuts
1 egg
2 teaspoons grated orange rind
¼ teaspoon salt
1 package (12 ounces) milk chocolate chips

Combine oats, sugar, oil, walnuts, egg, orange rind and salt in large bowl until blended. Cover; refrigerate overnight. Preheat oven to 350°F. Lightly grease cookie sheets or line with parchment paper. Melt chocolate chips in top of double boiler over hot, not boiling, water; set aside. Shape oat mixture into large-marble-sized balls. Place 2 inches apart on prepared cookie sheets. Bake 10 to 12 minutes or until golden and crisp. Cool 10 minutes on wire racks. Dip tops of cookies, one at a time, into melted chocolate. Place on waxed paper; cool until chocolate is set.

Makes about 6 dozen cookies

CHOCOLATE PISTACHIO FINGERS

Both ends of these buttery, finger-shaped cookies are dipped into melted chocolate. Then, for an elegant finish, the chocolate ends are covered with chopped pistachios.

¾ cup butter or margarine, softened
⅓ cup sugar
3 ounces (about ⅓ cup) almond paste
1 egg yolk
1⅔ cups all-purpose flour
1 cup (6 ounces) semisweet chocolate chips
½ cup finely chopped natural pistachios

Preheat oven to 350°F. Line cookie sheets with parchment paper or lightly grease and dust with flour. Cream butter and sugar in large bowl until blended. Add almond paste and egg yolk; beat until light. Blend in flour to make a smooth dough. (If dough is too soft to handle, cover and refrigerate until firm.) Turn out onto lightly floured board. Divide into 8 equal pieces; divide each piece in half. Roll each half into a 12-inch rope; cut each rope into 2-inch lengths. Place 2 inches apart on prepared cookie sheets. Bake 10 to 12 minutes or until edges just begin to brown. Remove to wire racks to cool. Melt chocolate chips in small bowl over hot water. Stir until smooth. Dip both ends of cookies about ½ inch into melted chocolate, then dip the chocolate ends into pistachios. Place on waxed paper; let stand until chocolate is set.

Makes 8 dozen cookies

PECAN FLORENTINES

Florentines are lacy confections that require a bit more skill than the average drop cookie. When baked on foil as directed, they are much easier to handle.

¾ cup pecan halves,
  pulverized*
½ cup all-purpose flour
⅓ cup packed brown sugar
¼ cup light corn syrup
¼ cup butter or margarine
2 tablespoons milk
⅓ cup semisweet chocolate
  chips

Preheat oven to 350°F. Line cookie sheets with foil; lightly grease foil. Combine pecans and flour in small bowl. Combine sugar, syrup, butter and milk in medium saucepan. Stir over medium heat until mixture comes to a boil. Remove from heat; stir in flour mixture. Drop batter by teaspoonfuls about 3 inches apart onto prepared cookie sheets. Bake 10 to 12 minutes or until lacy and golden brown. (Cookies are soft when hot, but become crispy as they cool.) Cool completely on foil. Place chocolate chips in small heavy-duty plastic bag; close securely. Set bag in bowl of hot water until chips are melted, being careful not to let any water into bag. (Knead bag lightly to check that chips are completely melted.) Pat bag dry. With scissors, snip off a small corner from one side of bag. Squeeze melted chocolate over cookies to decorate. Let stand until chocolate is set. Peel foil off cookies.

Makes about 3 dozen cookies

*To pulverize pecans, place in food processor or blender. Process until thoroughly ground with a dry, not pasty, texture.

TRIPLE CHOCOLATE PRETZELS

Buttery pretzel-shaped chocolate cookies are glazed with dark chocolate, then decorated with white chocolate for a triple chocolate treat.

2 squares (1 ounce each) unsweetened chocolate
½ cup butter or margarine, softened
½ cup granulated sugar
1 egg
2 cups cake flour
1 teaspoon vanilla
¼ teaspoon salt
   Mocha Glaze (recipe follows)
2 ounces white chocolate, chopped

Melt unsweetened chocolate in top of double boiler over hot, not boiling, water. Remove from heat; cool. Cream butter and granulated sugar in large bowl until light. Add egg and melted chocolate; beat until fluffy. Stir in cake flour, vanilla and salt until well blended. Cover; refrigerate until firm, about 1 hour.

Preheat oven to 400°F. Lightly grease cookie sheets or line with parchment paper. Divide dough into 4 equal parts. Divide each part into 12 pieces. To form pretzels, knead each piece briefly to soften dough. Roll into a rope about 6 inches long. Form each rope on prepared cookie sheet into a pretzel shape. Repeat with all pieces of dough, spacing cookies 2 inches apart. Bake 7 to 9 minutes or until firm. Remove to wire racks to cool. Prepare Mocha Glaze. Dip pretzels, one at a time, into glaze to coat completely. Place on waxed paper, right side up. Let stand until glaze is set. Melt white chocolate in small bowl over hot water. Squeeze melted chocolate through pastry bag or drizzle over pretzels to decorate. Let stand until chocolate is completely set.

Makes 4 dozen cookies

MOCHA GLAZE
1 cup (6 ounces) semisweet chocolate chips
1 teaspoon light corn syrup
1 teaspoon shortening
1 cup powdered sugar
3 to 5 tablespoons hot coffee or water

Combine chocolate chips, corn syrup and shortening in small heavy saucepan. Stir over low heat until chocolate is melted. Stir in powdered sugar and enough coffee to make a smooth glaze.

Top: Chocolate Spritz (page 88) and Chocolate Cherry Cookies (page 73), bottom: Triple Chocolate Pretzels

CHOCOLATE SPRITZ

2 squares (1 ounce each)
   unsweetened chocolate
1 cup butter, softened
½ cup granulated sugar
1 egg
1 teaspoon vanilla
¼ teaspoon salt
2¼ cups all-purpose flour
   Powdered sugar

Preheat oven to 400°F. Line cookie sheets with parchment paper or leave ungreased. Melt chocolate in top of double boiler over hot, not boiling, water. Remove from heat; cool. Cream butter, granulated sugar, egg, vanilla and salt in large bowl until light. Blend in melted chocolate and flour until stiff. Fit cookie press with your choice of plate. Load press with dough; press cookies out onto cookie sheets, spacing 2 inches apart. Bake 5 to 7 minutes or just until very slightly browned around edges. Remove to wire racks to cool. Dust with powdered sugar.

Makes about 5 dozen cookies

CHOCOLATE-FROSTED ALMOND SHORTBREAD

This shortbread keeps quite well in the refrigerator. Simply slip the whole pan into a plastic bag and seal securely.

¾ cup butter, softened
¼ cup packed light brown
   sugar
¼ cup powdered sugar
1 egg yolk
1 teaspoon almond extract
1½ cups all-purpose flour
⅛ teaspoon baking soda
7 ounces (about 1 cup)
   almond paste
½ cup granulated sugar
1 egg
½ cup milk chocolate chips

Preheat oven to 350°F. Cover bottom of a 9-inch pie pan with parchment or waxed paper. Cream butter, brown sugar, powdered sugar, egg yolk and almond extract in large bowl. Blend in flour and baking soda until smooth. Press half of the dough into prepared pie pan. Beat almond paste, granulated sugar and whole egg in small bowl until smooth. Spread over dough in pan. Roll out remaining half of dough on lightly floured surface into a circle to fit top of almond layer. Place over almond layer; press down to make smooth top. Bake 30 to 40 minutes or until top appears very lightly browned and feels firm. Remove from oven; sprinkle chocolate chips over the top. Let stand a few minutes until chips melt, then spread evenly over shortbread. Refrigerate until chocolate is set. Cut into slim wedges to serve.

Makes 16 to 20 cookies

DANISH RASPBERRY COOKIES

These fancy cookies look like you fussed all day making them. Only you know how easy and fun they were to prepare.

2 squares (1 ounce each) unsweetened chocolate
½ cup butter or margarine, softened
½ cup sugar
1 egg
2 cups cake flour
1 teaspoon vanilla
¼ teaspoon salt
1 cup (6 ounces) milk chocolate or white chocolate chips *or* ½ cup of each
1 to 1¼ cups seedless raspberry preserves or jam

Melt unsweetened chocolate in top of double boiler over hot, not boiling, water. Remove from heat; cool. Cream butter and sugar in large bowl until light. Add egg and melted chocolate; beat until fluffy. Stir in cake flour, vanilla and salt until well blended. Cover; refrigerate until firm, about 1 hour.

Preheat oven to 400°F. Lightly grease cookie sheets or line with parchment paper. Divide dough into 4 equal parts. Divide each part into 2 pieces. Roll each piece into a rope 12 inches long on lightly floured board. (The ropes should be about the thickness of a finger.) Place 2 inches apart on prepared cookie sheets. With side of finger, make an indentation along length of each rope. Bake 8 minutes or until firm. Meanwhile, melt chocolate chips in small bowl over hot water. Stir until smooth. (If using both kinds of chips, melt separately.) Stir preserves; spoon into pastry bag fitted with ¼-inch tip or into small heavy-duty plastic bag. (If using plastic bag, snip off a small corner from one side of bag.) Remove cookies from oven. Press preserves down length of each cookie strip. Return to oven for 2 minutes, then remove to wire racks. While cookies are still warm, drizzle melted chocolate over the tops, then cut strips into 1-inch diagonal pieces. Refrigerate until chocolate is set.

Makes 8 dozen cookies

CHOCOLATE COOKIE PRINTS

Cookie stamps imprint cookies with a raised design. Usually made of ceramic or glass, they are available in specialty shops or large department stores.

2 squares (1 ounce each)
  unsweetened chocolate
½ cup butter or margarine,
  softened
¾ cup sugar
1 egg
2 cups cake flour
1 teaspoon vanilla
¼ teaspoon salt
  Sugar

Melt chocolate in top of double boiler over hot, not boiling, water. Remove from heat; cool. Cream butter and sugar in large bowl until light. Add egg and melted chocolate; beat until fluffy. Stir in cake flour, vanilla and salt until well blended. Cover; refrigerate until firm, about 1 hour.

Preheat oven to 400°F. Lightly grease cookie sheets or line with parchment paper. Divide dough into 4 equal parts. Divide each part into 12 pieces. Roll each pieceintoasmoothroundball.Place2 inches apart on prepared cookie sheets. Dip cookie stamp into water, then into sugar. Press down firmly onto a dough ball; remove. (Cookie will have imprint of stamp on it.) Repeat for each cookie, dipping stamp into water and sugar each time. Bake 7 to 9 minutes or until firm. Remove to wire racks to cool.

Makes 4 dozen cookies

CHOCOLATE RUM BALLS

½ cup butter or margarine,
  softened
⅓ cup granulated sugar
1 egg yolk
1 tablespoon dark rum
1 teaspoon vanilla
1 cup all-purpose flour
¼ cup unsweetened cocoa
1 cup finely chopped
  walnuts or pecans
  Powdered sugar

Cream butter, granulated sugar and egg yolk in large bowl until light and fluffy. Blend in rum and vanilla. Stir in flour, cocoa and nuts; mix well. Cover; refrigerate until firm, about 1 hour. Preheat oven to 350°F. Lightly grease cookie sheets or line with parchment paper. Shape dough into 1-inch balls. Place 2 inches apart on prepared cookie sheets. Bake 15 to 20 minutes or until firm. Remove to wire racks to cool. Roll in powdered sugar.

Makes about 3 dozen cookies

Clockwise from center: Chocolate Tassies (page 93),
Chocolate-Dipped Almond Crescents (page 92), Chocolate Cookie Prints

CHOCOLATE-DIPPED ALMOND CRESCENTS

One end of these crescent-shaped cookies is dipped into melted chocolate—a decorative touch that makes them look special.

1 cup butter or margarine, softened
1 cup powdered sugar
2 egg yolks
2½ cups all-purpose flour
1½ teaspoons almond extract
1 cup (6 ounces) semisweet chocolate chips

Preheat oven to 375°F. Line cookie sheets with parchment paper or leave ungreased. Cream butter, sugar and egg yolks in large bowl. Beat in flour and almond extract until well mixed. Shape dough into 1-inch balls. (If dough is too soft to handle, cover and refrigerate until firm.) Roll balls into 2-inch long ropes, tapering both ends. Curve ropes into crescent shapes. Place 2 inches apart on cookie sheets. Bake 8 to 10 minutes or until set, but not browned. Remove to wire racks to cool. Melt chocolate chips in top of double boiler over hot, not boiling, water. Dip one end of each crescent in melted chocolate. Place on waxed paper; cool until chocolate is set.

Makes about 5 dozen cookies

COCOA GINGERBREAD COOKIES

¼ cup butter or margarine, softened
2 tablespoons shortening
⅓ cup packed brown sugar
¼ cup dark molasses
1 egg
1½ cups all-purpose flour
¼ cup unsweetened cocoa
½ teaspoon baking soda
½ teaspoon ground ginger
½ teaspoon ground cinnamon
¼ teaspoon salt
¼ teaspoon ground nutmeg
⅛ teaspoon ground cloves
Decorator Icing (page 79)

Preheat oven to 400°F. Lightly grease cookie sheets or line with parchment paper. Cream butter, shortening, brown sugar and molasses in large bowl. Add egg; beat until light. Combine flour, cocoa, baking soda, ginger, cinnamon, salt, nutmeg and cloves in small bowl. Blend into creamed mixture until smooth. (If dough is too soft to handle, cover and refrigerate until firm.) Roll out dough ¼ inch thick on lightly floured surface. Cut out with cookie cutters. Place 2 inches apart on prepared cookie sheets. Bake 8 to 10 minutes or until firm. Remove to wire racks to cool. Prepare Decorator Icing. Spoon into pastry bag fitted with small tip. Decorate cookies with icing.

Makes about 6 dozen cookies

CHOCOLATE TASSIES

Tassies are old-fashioned cookies that resemble miniature pecan tarts. Here, the pecan filling is enriched with chocolate.

PASTRY
- 2 cups all-purpose flour
- 2 packages (3 ounces each) cream cheese, cold, cut into chunks
- 1 cup butter or margarine, cold, cut into chunks

FILLING
- 2 tablespoons butter or margarine
- 2 squares (1 ounce each) unsweetened chocolate
- 1½ cups packed brown sugar
- 2 teaspoons vanilla
- 2 eggs, beaten
- Dash salt
- 1½ cups chopped pecans

To prepare Pastry: Place flour in large bowl. Cut in cream cheese and butter. Continue to mix until dough can be shaped into a ball. Wrap dough in plastic wrap; refrigerate 1 hour. Shape dough into 1-inch balls. Press each ball into ungreased miniature (1¾-inch) muffin pan cup, covering bottom and side of cup with dough. Preheat oven to 350°F.

To prepare Filling: Melt butter and chocolate in medium-sized heavy saucepan over low heat. Remove from heat. Blend in sugar, vanilla, eggs and salt; beat until thick. Stir in pecans. Spoon about 1 teaspoon filling into each unbaked pastry shell. Bake 20 to 25 minutes or until lightly browned and filling is set. Cool in pans on wire racks. Remove from pans; store in airtight containers.

Makes about 5 dozen cookies

ALMOND FUDGE CUPS

PASTRY
- ¾ cup butter or margarine, softened
- ⅓ cup sugar
- 2 cups all-purpose flour
- 1 tablespoon almond- or fruit-flavored liqueur *or* water
- 1 teaspoon vanilla

FILLING
- 1 cup (6 ounces) semisweet chocolate chips
- ¾ cup blanched almonds
- 2 eggs
- ½ cup sugar
- Dash salt

To prepare Pastry: Lightly grease 3 dozen miniature (1¾-inch) muffin pan cups or small tart shells. Cream butter and sugar in large bowl until blended. Add flour, liqueur and vanilla; stir to make moist crumbs. Divide crumbs evenly among muffin cups; press to cover bottoms and sides of cups completely. Preheat oven to 350°F.

To prepare Filling: Place chocolate chips and almonds in food processor or blender. Process until finely ground. Beat eggs in medium bowl until thick; stir in sugar and salt. Blend in chocolate mixture. Spoon filling into unbaked pastry shells. Bake 20 minutes or until filling is set. Cool in pans on wire racks. Store in airtight containers.

Makes 3 dozen cookies

CHOCOLATE-FROSTED MARSHMALLOW COOKIES

COOKIES

- ½ cup butter or margarine
- 2 squares (1 ounce each) unsweetened chocolate
- 1 egg
- 1 cup packed brown sugar
- 1 teaspoon vanilla
- ½ teaspoon baking soda
- 1½ cups all-purpose flour
- ½ cup milk
- 1 package (16 ounces) large marshmallows, halved crosswise

FROSTING

- 1½ squares (1½ ounces) unsweetened chocolate
- ¼ cup butter or margarine
- 1½ cups powdered sugar
- 1 egg white*
- 1 teaspoon vanilla

To prepare Cookies: Preheat oven to 350°F. Lightly grease cookie sheets or line with parchment paper. Melt butter and chocolate in small heavy saucepan over low heat; stir to blend. Remove from heat; cool. Beat egg, brown sugar, vanilla and baking soda in large bowl until light and fluffy. Blend in chocolate mixture and flour until smooth. Slowly beat in milk to make a light, cake-batter-like dough. Drop dough by teaspoonfuls 2 inches apart onto prepared cookie sheets. Bake 10 to 12 minutes or until firm in center. Immediately place a halved marshmallow, cut side down, onto each baked cookie. Return to oven 1 minute or just until marshmallow is warm enough to stick to cookie. Remove to wire racks to cool.

To prepare Frosting: Melt chocolate and butter in small heavy saucepan over low heat; stir to blend. Beat in powdered sugar. Beat in egg white and vanilla, adding a little water, if necessary, to make a smooth, slightly soft frosting. Spoon frosting over cookies to cover marshmallows.

Makes about 5 dozen cookies

*Use clean, uncracked egg.

I N D E X